HOW TO MAKE
BEAUTIFUL FLOWERS

HOW TO MAKE
BEAUTIFUL FLOWERS

SEARCH PRESS LIMITED

First published in Great Britain 1984 by
Search Press Limited
Wellwood, North Farm Road
Tunbridge Wells, Kent TN2 3DR.

Copyright © Search Press 1984

Edited by Valerie Jackson
Designed by David Stanley

The chapters of this book are based on the following individual
volumes previously published in the *Leisure Crafts* series (Search
Press) and the *Brunnen-Reihe* series (Christophorus-Verlag,
Freiburg):

Silk and fabric flowers: *Kunstvolle Seidenblumen* (BR174) and
Hauchzarte Seidenblumen (BR164) by Teresa Shang Mui Wan,
translated by Ivan Houghton; photos by Toni Schneiders and
Ulrike Schneiders. Copyright Christophorus Verlag © 1981 and
1980 respectively.

Shell flowers: *Sea Shells* by Maxine Fitter. Part used in *Nature-craft*
copyright © Search Press 1979. Also *Muschel-Spieleseien* (BR122)
by Hans Fasold, photos by Toni Schneiders. Copyright ©
Christophorous Verlag 1977.

Bread dough flowers: *Mexican bread dough sculpture* by Sheila
Franklin. Not yet published separately.

Paper flowers (LC42) by Beryle Bell, photos by Robert Harding:
copyright © Search Press 1973. Translated into German as
Partyblumen aus Papier (BR106) by Eleonore Hüni with
additional designs by Elisabeth Hammer and photos by Toni
Schneiders. German text and photos copyright © Christophorus
Verlag 1975. Also *Papierfiguren* (BR52) by Arthur Sadler,
copyright © Blandford Press Ltd., 1964, 1965, German translation
by Gabriele C. Pallat, copyright © Christophorus Verlag 1969.

Feather flowers: *Feathercraft* (LC56) by Pamela Woods. Photos by
John Morfett. Copyright © Search Press 1976.

Seed flowers: *Fun with seeds* (LC47) by Ruth Phelps, photos by
Jeet Jain, copyright © Search Press 1975; *Blumen aus Kernen und
Körner* (BR184), photos by Ulrike Schneiders, copyright ©
Christophorus Verlag 1978; *Kerne und Körner* (BR131) by Doris
Epple, photos by Toni Schneiders, copyright © Christophorus
Verlag 1978.

Fantasies in plastic (LC48) by Eric Jenner and others, photographs
by Robert Harding, copyright © Search Press 1975. *Zauberhaftes
aus Tauchlack* (BR129) by Margret Glende, photos by Toni
Schneiders, copyright © Christophorus Verlag 1977.

Nylon flowers: *Nylon flowers* (LC68) by Hazel Chitty, photographs
by John Wyand, copyright © Search Press 1978; *Blumenzauber
aus Draht und Strümpfen* by Elfreide d'Amato (BR134), photos
and drawings by Alfred Kutschera, copyright © Christophorus
Verlag 1978; *Blütenzauber aus Draht und Strümpfen* (BR169) by
Ingeborg Westphal. Photos by Toni Schneiders, copyright ©
Christophorus Verlag 1980.

ISBN (UK) 0 85532 523 2

Printed in Spain in Elkar S. Coop, Bilbao-12

CONTENTS

Note on measurements: Since the dimensions and measurements given in the book are mostly small, they have been given in centimetres and millimetres rather than inches. There are 2½ centimetres, or 25 millimetres, to 1 inch.

SILK FLOWERS

SILK FLOWERS

The most beautiful of nature's flowers can be charmingly re-created in silk and other materials to provide long-lasting and exotic arrangements for the home or to serve as unusual dress accessories.

The techniques of flower-making in fabric are not difficult to master and the tools and equipment needed are readily available. This is a craft which will give you hours of pleasure as it introduces you to a new artistic skill and gives you fresh insight into the world of flowers.

Tools required for flower-making

Scissors. Floral scissors are especially designed to cut both wire and fabric but you can substitute a pair of heavy scissors for wire and a finer pair for fabric. The points of the scissors are used to crease the petals.
Awl. Pierce the centre of the calyces and petals with a small, straight awl. This can also be used for curling the edges of the petals by rolling them over the thin metal shaft.
Tweezers. Helpful for handling petals.
Knife, fork, spoon. For ironing the curves into petals, putting veins in leaves and for shaping floral components. Heat the appropriate end of the tool in the flame of a small spirit burner. Bend the spoon to a right angle and squeeze the prongs of the fork together to make them easier to use. (You can also buy an electric soldering iron, especially made to shape and crease the petals of fabric flowers, and mark veins on petals and leaves.)
Small spirit burner. For heating tools.
Foam rubber pad. A pad of thick foam rubber covered with thin cotton is used as a base for ironing. This prevents the fabric tearing and controls the pressure of the iron when curving petals and marking veins.

Materials for flower-making

Most fine fabrics, including silk, rayon, velveteen, satin and georgette are suitable for flower-making, but it is worth experimenting with other fabrics. All fabrics, however, except those pretreated must be treated with starch and glue solution in order to prevent the edges fraying, to preserve the shape of the petals and leaves, and to keep the fabric looking fresh. looking fresh.
Japanese floral ribbon. Pre-treated fabric ribbons, made especially for flower-making, are produced in Japan. These do not fray and need no starching. They come in myriad colours, both plain and shaded (ombre), and in many textures such as organza, satin, cotton and velveteen.
Floral tape. Self-adhesive tape, available in many colours, is wound around wire to make stems. Floral tape is available in 12.5mm widths but a better result is obtained if it is cut in half (6.25mm) and stretched before use. Wind it round in an even spiral with the edges just overlapping. Stems can also be covered with paper tape or with glued strips of fabric.
Double-sided adhesive tape. Transparent film with adhesive on both sides is sometimes used for fastening parts of flowers and fabric together. It is obtainable in 5mm and 10mm widths.
Cotton thread. To make the centres of some flowers.
Stamens. Stamens are made by stiffening cotton thread with starch, cutting it into suitable lengths (about 10mm) and adding a blob of glue to the end of each thread. The resulting shape resembles a match head. Ready-made stamens can also be bought cheaply from craft shops in most shapes, sizes and colours.
Cotton wool. Cotton wool is used to pad buds, as flower centres, and for shaping the base of some calyces and flowers.
Wires. Steel wire is the foundation of the stems and a support for leaves and petals. The gauge used varies with the size of each flower but the most commonly used sizes are 18, 22, 24, 26, and 30 Standard Wire Gauge (SWG). The higher the number, the finer the wire.
Tissue paper. Wrapped around wire to pad out stems.
Decorative ribbon. Fancy ribbons and ties are attractive additions to bouquets and corsages.
Adhesive. Quick-drying adhesive which dries clear is an important requirement (UHU or Bostick 1).
Colouring. Felt-tipped pens, coloured chalks or fabric paints provide shading, highlights and vein markings.
Starch. Use ordinary laundry starch dissolved in boiling water (see Basic techniques below).
Other items. Ruler, paint brushes.

Basic techniques of flower-making

How to starch
Always starch material before cutting out any patterns. Mix one tablespoonful of starch with a tablespoonful of cold water to form a smooth paste. Boil four-fifths of a cup of water and add the starch paste to it. Boil the solution over a low flame and stir constantly until it thickens. Remove the solution from the heat and add a table-spoonful of clear white soluble glue. Mix this in and allow the mixture to cool.

Stake out the material to be treated with drawing pins on a smooth board, and reverse side upwards. The board must be kept flat. Apply the starch with a paint brush, and remove any excess with a moist cloth. Ensure that there are no air bubbles or creases in the fabric. Allow the fabric to dry thoroughly.

Petal structure
(The vertical gathering method)
Glue a white-covered wire inside a half-folded petal

Crocus and snowdrops. Spring crocus and snowdrops are displayed here in an imaginative container which is simply made of wire and floral tape, in the shape of a small cart. The carefully chosen colours of pale yellow, white and green are especially suitable for a spring-like arrangement. See also text, page 28–9.

and smooth the edge with a ruler (*Diagram A, overleaf*). When it is dry, open the petal and re-fold it in the opposite direction. Place it inside a folded handkerchief, press it firmly with your left palm and pull the right side of the handkerchief slowly until it passes your left hand. Open the petal and you will find it is evenly creased both sides.

Making a flower
The petals are joined to the stem of calyx. Hold one end of a fine (30SWG) wire with the left forefinger and

9

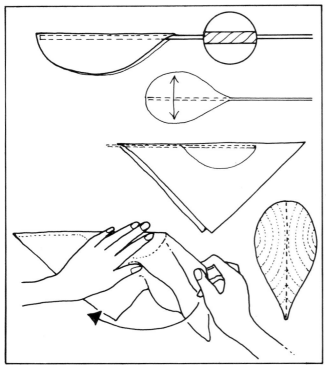

Diagram A

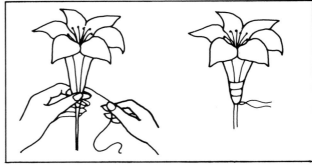

Diagram B

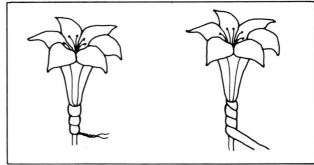

Diagram C

thumb together with the petals and stem. Hold the other end of the wire in the right hand and bind the flower components together by winding the wire around them three times, pulling, then twisting tightly three or four times. (*Diagram B*).

Lengthening and thickening stems

Stems can be lengthened, thickened or strengthened by adding a thick wire to the stem. Secure them by binding with 30SWG wire and cover by winding green floral tape around it. To thicken still further, 10mm wide strips of tissue paper can be wound around the stem and stuck with glue. The whole can then be covered with floral tape.

Covering a stem

Wrap floral tape round the stem twice and hold it with the left thumb and forefinger. Stretch the tape with the right hand and pull it downwards while rotating the wire stems in order to cover the wire (*Diagram C*).

Dyeing

Much greater realism can be achieved by careful colouring. For dyeing you will need: fabric dyes or paints; liquid detergent (two drops to half a cupful of water); fine paint brushes; blotting paper; cotton wool; tweezers.

How to work

If you are using powered dye, put a little of it on a dish and dissolve it by mixing in some boiling water. To deepen the colour, mix in more dark dye; to lighten the colour, dilute with more water.

When dyeing thin materials, place several petals one on top of the other and dip them into the detergent solution. With a pair of tweezers remove the petals, separate them and place them on the blotting paper. When the excess fluid has been absorbed, place the petals on top of each other again and dip them into the dye solution. Once again, remove the petals, separate them and dry on blotting paper. If the petals are to be multi-coloured, darker shades can be painted on, as can veins and other markings.

When dyeing thick materials, moisten petals or leaves with cotton wool dipped in detergent solution, then brush the dye on to the petals and dry thoroughly.

The edges of the petals alone can be dyed by, first, moistening their edges with detergent solution, then dipping them in the dye solution.

Painting. Fabric paints are readily available and are easier to prepare than dyes. They can be mixed to change colours, or diluted to lighten them. To fix fabric paints and for long-lasting results, you must iron the fabric after applying the paints. Use an electric iron or heated spoon. For realistic-looking results, it is best to copy directly from real flowers, but if that is not possible, use coloured photographs or work from a good reference book.

Orchid, Tiger lily and Day lily. *Deep plum-coloured orchids, tiger lilies from the Orient and lemon-yellow day lilies make up this charming bowl of flowers. Day lilies also come in orange, pink or dark red, all with the characteristic of long, ribbon-like leaves.*

Shaping petals and veining leaves

The beautiful shape of a flower comes from the curves and hollows of the petals. To re-create them, heat a small teaspoon in the flame of a spirit burner. Place the petal on the cotton-covered foam block and press the heated bowl of the spoon firmly on the petal.

The edges of the petals can then be curled in the same way. To mark veins in petals, heat a butter curler or a fork (its prongs squeezed together). Use the back of a heated knife blade to iron in the veins of leaves. For small hollows, heat the rounded end of a metal handle. Curve the calyx and long leaves or petals by holding the base of the leaf or petal, then firmly drawing it over the blunt edge of a scissor or knife blade.

(Lily and) Tiger Lily

Flowers. Organza, silk or thin cotton.
Petals. 10cm × 3cm. Six orange petals per flower, with black spots concentrated mainly in the centre.
Leaves. 9cm × 1.5cm, three per flower, green cotton or satin.
Stamens. Seven, painted orange with black spots.

How to work

Cut out and dye all the petals and leaves. Make the top and bottom of the petals a shade darker. Use a fine paint brush or felt-tipped pen to paint black spots on the petals and curl the edges of the petals by ironing them. Glue a 24SWG orange-painted wire along the back of each petal to support it.

Cut wires for the stamens and pistil into 15cm lengths and attach a stamen head and pistil head to the top of each with green floral tape.

Bend the heads at right angles and join the stamens and pistil at their base with 30SWG wire covered with green floral tape. The long green pistil extends about 2.5cm beyond the stamens.

11

Arrange the petals round the centre with the stamens above the petals and secure with 30SWG wire and green floral tape. Bend the petals over backwards to give them their characteristic curved shape.

Mark the leaf veins with the back of a heated knife blade and glue a green wire to the back. Fasten leaves to the stems of flowers.

Make Day lilies the same way but arrange the petals so that they form trumpet shapes, and add no spots. Lilies and Tiger lilies, with their long green leaves, make an attractive arrangement together.

Peonies. *These large, flamboyant flowers, with their unusual dark spikey leaves, are surprisingly simple to construct and can make a dramatic contribution to a festive table. They also look good in other, darker colours.*

Peony

Flowers. Organza or georgette for petals and buds (use ombre organza, the darker part towards the base).

Petals. 6cm × 9cm, ten per flower;
5cm × 8cm, six per flower;
7cm × 7cm, one per bud.

Leaves. Satin or cotton.
7.2cm × 10.5cm (large);
6cm × 7cm (small);

Calyx. Satin or cotton.
3cm × 3cm.

Stamens. 30 medium-sized yellow stamens per flower; 50 white stamens per flower.

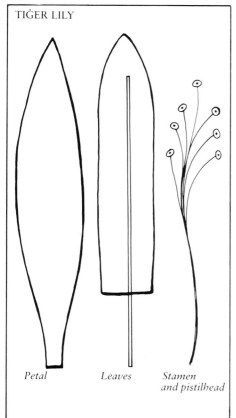

TIGER LILY

Petal

Leaves

Stamen
and pistilhead

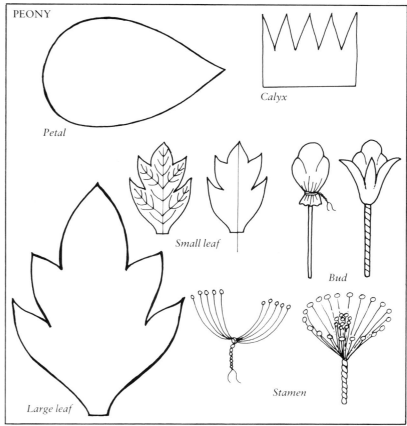

PEONY

Petal

Calyx

Small leaf

Bud

Large leaf

Stamen

How to work

Cut the peony leaves and petals as in the diagram. Hollow the centre of the petals with a heated spoon and curl the edges with the blade of a heated knife, as shown in the photographs overleaf, which apply to peony petals just as much as to the rose petals and leaves which are shown.

To make the centre of the flower, gather 30 medium-sized yellow stamens and tie them together with 30SWG wire and cover in green floral tape. Make five bundles, each of ten white stamens and secure them with wire and green tape. Attach them round the yellow stamens so that they project above the central yellow stamens by 1.5cm. Cover the join with green tape.

Arrange the smaller petals evenly round the centre of the flower and glue them in place. Arrange the outer layer petals round and alternately with the inner layer petals and glue them in place. Cover the base of the flower in green tape.

To make a bud, bend the end of a 24SWG green-covered wire to form a hook and glue on a small cotton wool ball. Cover the ball with a square of fabric and secure it by binding with 30SWG wire. Cover the joins with green floral tape.

Curl the edges of the calyx outwards by rubbing it over the edges of the scissors, then glue a 24SWG wire on the back of each leaf.

Extend the stem by joining on an 18SWG green-covered wire and attach leaves and buds to the stem with green floral tape.

Picture 1

Picture 2

Picture 3

Picture 4

Picture 5

Picture 6

Making a rose

Picture 1. **Shaping the petals.** After they have been cut out, petals will look more natural if they are hollowed. Heat a small spoon (its bowl bent at right angles to the handle) in the flame of a spirit burner. Place the petal on a cotton-covered piece of foam and gently press the spoon firmly on the petal.

Picture 2. **Curving the end of a petal.** To get a naturalistic curve in the end of a petal (or in a calyx or long leaf) hold the base of the petal over the blunt end of a knife and draw the petal firmly over the edge until the petal curls. The blade of a pair of scissors will also have the same effect.

Picture 3. **Marking veins on leaves.** Rose leaves will look much more realistic if they have vein markings on them. Heat the back of a knife blade to mark the veins in rose leaves (or some flower petals, if they require this detail). The heat of the knife combined with the pressure on the fabric will ensure that the veins stay ironed-in.

Picture 4. **Covering a stem.** Hold the floral tape firmly with the left thumb and forefinger and wrap the tape round the stem twice, stretching the tape with the right hand and pulling it downwards while rotating the wire stem. This makes for a smooth, even covering that will not unwind at a later stage and spoil the look of the flower.

Picture 5. **Attaching petals.** Make a small hook in the covered wire and glue a small ball of cotton wool to it. Then glue a petal around this to cover it. Add two more petals on either side, then the outer petals, hollowed out as in Picture 1. Rose petals also have their outer edges curled, for more realism.

Picture 6. **Finishing the rose.** Cut out the leaves, which are shaped like those of a peony, and make vein marks as in Picture 3. Attach the leaves to the wire stem with floral tape, binding it securely so that there is no likelihood of it coming away from the stem. The number of leaves can be varied to choice.

14

Yellow roses

Flowers. Satin or organza.
Petals. Inner, 5.5cm × 4cm, three per flower;
         Outer, 6.8cm × 5.5cm, nine per flower.
Calyx. Satin. 5cm × 8cm, one per flower.
Leaves. Satin. 6cm × 3.5cm (large);
         5cm × 3cm (small);
Bud.   5.5cm × 4cm, three per flower.

How to work

Hollow the bud petals with a heated teaspoon on the underneath side, as shown on page 14, until creases appear at the edges. See also Rose pattern, page 18.

Yellow roses. *Roses are the most popular of all flowers, their shape and colours beloved by flower arrangers and gardeners all over the world. These are made in yellow satin, the sheen of the satin producing a variety of highlights without need of additional colour.*

Make a small hook with 18SWG wire and stick a small ball of cotton wool to it. Glue a petal around this to cover it, as shown in picture 5 on page 14 and then glue two further petals on each side. Glue the calyx and secure the base to the stem with green floral tape.

15

The inside of the rose is made with small petals in the same way as the bud, but leaving out the calyx. Hollow the centre front of the petals (as in the stippled area of the diagram on page 18). Refer to Picture 1 on page 14 for the hollowing-out process.

Turn the petals the other way up and curl the edges inwards at the shaded area of the diagram on page 18. Attach the middle layer petals around the centre and glue them in place with the edges turning outwards, then similarly add an outer layer of large petals.

Stick the calyx in place around the base of the flower. Cut out the leaves. Vein them and attach them to the wire stem, as in Picture 6, page 14.

Carnation

Flowers. Fine fabric such as organza or georgette.
Petals. 7.2cm × 7.2cm, seven per flower.
Calyx. Satin. 3cm × 4cm, one per flower.
Leaves. Satin. 1cm × 3cm, in pairs, four per flower.

How to work

Fold a 7.2cm square of petal material diagonally three times to make a triangle eight layers thick. Cut around the top open edge to make a segment of a circle and cut down each radial edge to a depth of 2cm. Make a 3cm cut in the rounded edge, then cut out a ragged edge in between (see cutting diagram).

Hollow out the petals at the shaded area of the diagram with a heated knife handle. (Each individual petal has one hollowed from the front and the other from the reverse side.) Fold three petals in half so that the backs of the petals protrude above between the front ones.

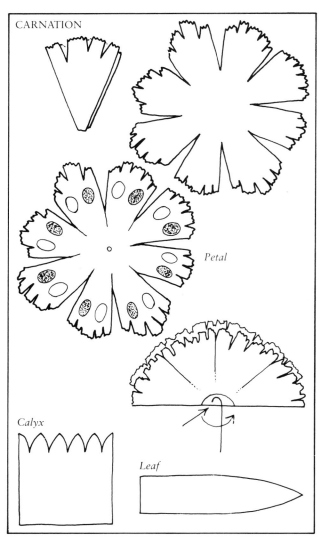

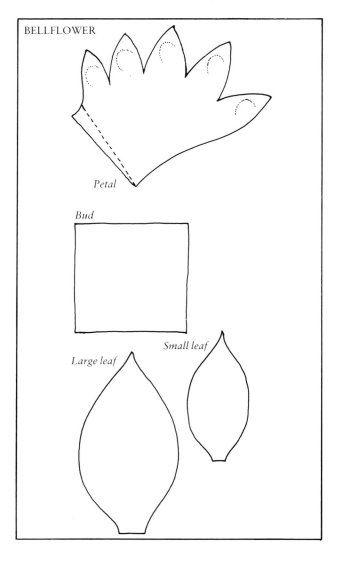

The next four layers of petals are made similarly but are not folded.

Glue a hook of 18swg wire in the middle of the folded petals, then fold again into four. Pierce a hole in the centre of the four unfolded petals and thread them over the stem. Glue to the centre.

Thicken the top of the stem with tissue paper and secure it with glue. Cut five little arches on the top edge of the calyx and curl them outwards. Glue around the thickened base of the flower.

Make narrow, pointed leaves with green wires glued to the backs. Fix to the stem by binding with green tape.

Carnations and bellflowers. *The special characteristic of the carnation is its notched and crinkled edge. It comes in many colours, but here yellow carnations are teamed with blue bellflowers to form a most effective combination.*

Bellflower

These are made of thin material such as organza, with four small yellow stamens per flower. Cut as in the diagram, curling the petals outwards with a heated knife. Bind to wires and cut leaves as for peony leaves.

Red roses. *Note how the edges of the outer petals of these red satin roses are folded outwards. You can increase the size of the flowers by increasing the number of petals. The gently curved bracts of the calyx show up clearly in the picture.*

Red roses

Flowers. Red satin.
Petals. Inner, 5.5cm × 4cm;
Outer, 6.8cm × 5.5cm, six per flower.
Calyx. Satin. 5cm × 8cm, one per flower.
Leaves. Satin. 6cm × 3.5cm (large);
5cm × 3cm (small).
Bud. 5.5cm × 4cm, three per flower.

How to work

Follow the instructions as for the yellow roses on page 15–16, but note that only six petals for each flower are required, not nine. See also the caption above.

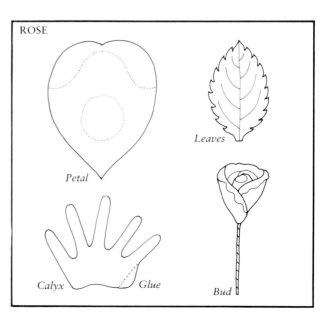

ROSE

Petal

Leaves

Calyx   Glue

Bud

Wild rose

Flowers. A mixture of satin and organza.
Petals. 6.5cm × 6.5cm, two of organza, one of satin, per flower.
Ovary. 2.5cm × 9cm, one per flower. Velveteen.
Bud. 3.5cm × 3.5cm, organza.
Calyx. 2.5cm × 1.8cm.

How to work

Cut the petals as shown overleaf. Pierce a hole in the centre of the petals and hollow them with a heated spoon on the upperside until creases appear at the edges. Make the centre or ovary of the flower from a strip of velveteen folded in half lengthwise. Apply a strip of double-sided adhesive tape along one edge on the reverse side to enable the edges to stick together.

Wild rose. *This posy could be an ornament on a silver salver, a table decoration, or a souvenir of a special evening for each guest. It would also make an attractive accessory for a plain dress or an evening gown, one that could be used on more than a single occasion.*

Cut the velveteen into strips, starting at the folded edge and cutting most of the way towards the adhesive tape. Bend a 24SWG wire into a hook at one end and hook it over the stuck edge between the strips on the right-hand side. Apply glue along the edge lengthways and wind the velveteen around the wire, then stick down with glue. This will form the centre.

Thread shaped petals through the stem from underneath. Glue the inner organza layer on to the centre. Follow this with another organza layer, the

19

first layer of petals showing between the gaps in the second. Glue the satin layer to the other layers and finally stick on a green calyx.

Vein and make leaves as for the peony.

To make buds, make a small wire hook and stick to it a ball of cotton wool. Cover the cotton wool with organza and bind it on to a stem.

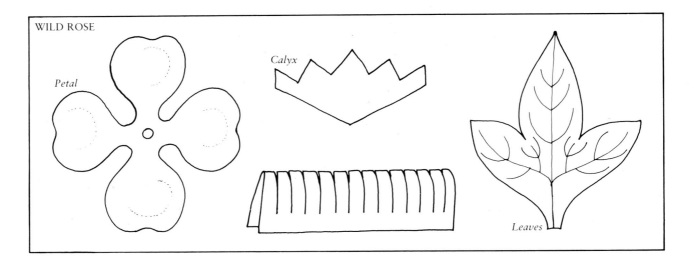

Poppy

Flowers. Organza.
Petals. 5cm × 7cm, four per flower.
Centre. 5cm × 5cm, one per flower, light green organza.
Leaves. 7cm × 5cm, two per flowers, cotton or satin.
Stamens. Thirty black stamens per flower.

How to work

Cut out and dye or paint the petals if necessary. If scarlet material is used, only the black markings at the base of the petals will have to be painted and for this a black, felt-tipped pen is ideal (see the diagram for the area to paint black). The petals must be ironed with a heated knife handle where stippled in the diagram, in order to make them 'bowl' realistically.

To make the seed box, form a hook by bending an 18SWG wire over and glueing on a small ball of cotton wool. Cover this with the square of pale green material and bind with 30SWG wire.

Cut three pieces of green 24SWG wire 6cm long and bend them over the seed box, securing them with glue on the top, to represent the markings of the poppy seed box. Secure the base with 30SWG wire and green floral tape.

Arrange the black stamens all around the centre in small bundles and secure them firmly at the base of the stem wire with wire and floral tape.

Glue the petals, one each side of the centre, to form the inner layer and space the other two between the inner layer petals to form the outer layer. Make the leaves as for peony leaves, and attach them to the poppy stems by binding with green tape.

Arrange the completed flowers in a Plasticine base.

Poppies. *A basket of scarlet poppies, as lovely as the real thing but much longer lasting. Here they are made in scarlet organza but in the picture on page 28 they are seen in shades of sepia and pale orange.*

Chrysanthemum

Flowers. Lantern ribbon.
Petals. Strip of ribbon, 7cm wide × 8cm long.
Bud. Strip of ribbon, 7cm side × 6cm long.
Centre. Strip of velveteen, 2.5cm wide × 7cm long.
Leaves. Velvet or satin, 3cm × 4cm.

How to work

Make the centre of the Chrysanthemums on stems as described for the Wild rose (pages 19–20).

Attach a strip of double-sided adhesive tape along one narrow edge of the strip of lantern ribbon, on the reverse side. Fold the strip in half lengthwise, and secure it to itself with the other side of the double-sided adhesive tape. Attach another small strip of double-sided adhesive tape to the base of the strip of

21

Chrysanthemums. *Late-blooming chrysanthemums are a welcome addition to autumn gardens, loved for their brilliant colours and pungeant fragrance. Here, pre-cut Lantern ribbon has been used to make a small posy.*

lantern ribbon and wind the ribbon round the edge of the velvet centre. Finish the flower by winding floral tape around the base. (Glue can be used instead of the double-sided tape.)

Make a bud by winding a strip of lantern ribbon around a hook of 24 SWG wire in the same way as the flower, but leaving out the centre. Attach leaves, as in the diagram, to complete the posy.

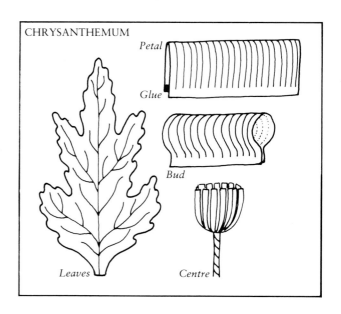

CHRYSANTHEMUM

Petal

Glue

Bud

Leaves

Centre

Slipper plant

Flowers. Organza or thin cotton. Small, 5cm × 3cm; medium, 7cm × 4cm; large, 9cm × 5cm.
Centres. Four small stamens per flower.
Calyx. 1.8cm × 1.8cm green cotton.
Leaves. Green cotton. Small, 5cm × 3cm; medium, 9cm × 6cm; large, 12cm × 8cm.

How to work

Using double material, cut out the flowers in the different sizes, as in the diagram on the next page. . Paint the markings in vermilion paint.

Cut the top of one half of the petal so that it forms an attached half circle, which can be folded inwards to form the characteristic shape of the slipper plant, with its purse-shaped blooms. Fold the half circle inwards. Iron the petals with a heated knife handle to pouch the

Slipper plant. This unusual and attractive rock plant from South America comes in many colours. The one shown here is a hybrid grown as a house plant, with yellow flowers, shaped like open pouches, which are spotted with vermilion.

flowers and hollow out the top. One or two lengths of fine wire glued to the underneath of the slipper will help to shape it. Fold the two halves together to form a purse-shaped flower and glue the edges together except at the top.

Gather four small stamens together and secure them with 30 SWG wire. Cover all but the heads of stamens with green tape.

23

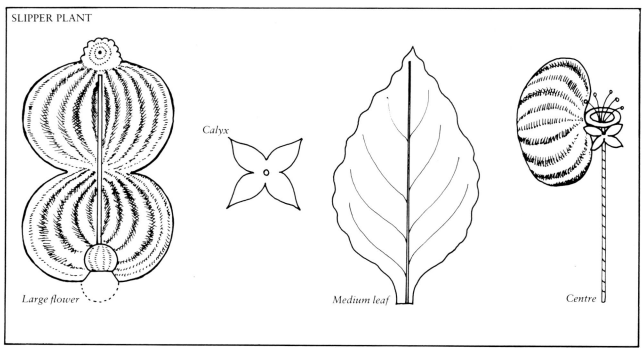

SLIPPER PLANT

Calyx

Large flower

Medium leaf

Centre

Push these through a hole already made at the top centre of the calyx and attach to the base of the centre. The more flowers you add, the more colourful the plant will look.

Paint yellow veins on the leaves to make them more realistic. Use a hot knife blade to mark in veins and to crease the edges. Glue support wires to the back of the leaves.

Attach small flowers and leaves to an 18SWG green-covered wire to form a branch. Add a few more, smaller branches and arrange large leaves at the base. Secure plant and leaves in a Plasticine base.

Hippeastrum or Amaryllis

Flowers. Red organza or cotton. Bracts, yellow or green organza.

Petals. Small, outer, 10cm × 5.5cm; small inner, 9cm × 4cm; large, outer, 11.5cm × 7cm; large inner 10.5cm × 5.5cm. (Three inner and three outer petals per flower.)

Buds. Six small inner layer petals per bud.

Leaves. 30cm × 5cm, but vary the sizes. Satin, or cotton.

Stems. 30cm × 2.5cm but vary the lengths. Satin or cotton.

Bracts. 5.5cm × 1.5cm, five per stem.

Stamens. Nine small yellow, per flower or bud.

How to work

Cut out all the petals as in the diagram, and leaves Mix red and black paint to make dark red and paint

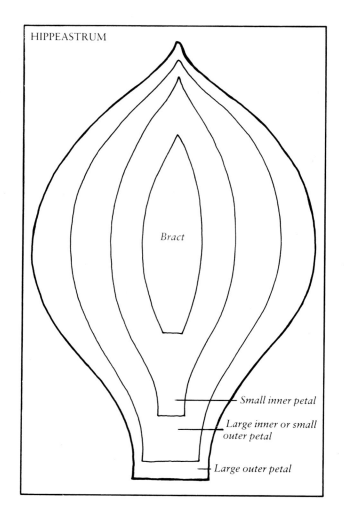

HIPPEASTRUM

Bract

Small inner petal

Large inner or small outer petal

Large outer petal

the base of the petals and their veins. When paint is dry, curl the edges of the petals by ironing with a heated knife handle. Cover a 22SWG wire in red floral tape and stick a length of it to the centre back of each petal.

Shade the leaves with yellow paint and glue 24SWG green support wires to the back. Paint the stamens green. Make a pistil from three stamens fastened together in a triangle. Gather stamens and pistil with the pistil projecting higher than the stamens and 2cm beyond the petals. Secure with fine wire and cover the base with green floral tape.

Arrange the three inner petals around the centre, then the three outer petals between them. Secure all six petals with green-covered wire. Then attach the flower to an 18SWG wire with fine wire and cover the

Hippeastrum. A group of hippeastrum makes a large and impressive arrangement. The exotic flowers come in red, pink or white trumpets, flowering in late winter or spring. The stems bear any number of flowers, from one to five.

join with green tape. Glue the five bracts around the stem near the base of the flower.

Thicken the stem by wrapping tissue paper around the wire until it is about 2cm thick, then bind with stem fabric and glue. Bend the flowers forward slightly, and arrange the bud petals in a closed position.

Sunflower

Flowers. Yellow cotton.
Petals. 7.2cm × 42cm, one per flower.
Bud. 7.2cm × 21cm, one per bud.
Leaves. 13cm × 6.5cm. Green cotton. Vary the sizes.
Calyx. 11cm × 11cm, one per flower, one per bud.
Green.
Stamens. Thirty, brown, per flower.

How to work

Fold the length of petal material four times and cut it
into strips, which are attached at their base, to make a
total of thirty-two petals per flower. Trim the ends to
make pointed petal shapes. Cut leaves.

Shade the petals with slightly darker yellow paint
and paint the veins in orange. Curl the petals outwards with a heated knife handle.

*Sunflowers. These large, radiant sunflowers bring a
touch of summer to any arrangement, but they need
a lot of support as the heads are heavy. An ideal
decoration for a dark corner of a room, perhaps
standing in a big vase on the floor.*

Cover a 28SWG wire in yellow fabric and glue it to
the back of each petal to support it. In the same way,
glue a 24SWG green wire to the back of each leaf.

Dye cotton wool dark brown and wind it around a
large hook made of two 18SWG wires bound together
to make a disc 7.5cm diameter, 2cm thick. Arrange
the stamens around the disc and secure them with
30SWG wire.

Glue the petals around the circumference of the disc and cut off the excess after one complete revolution. Then glue on the surplus petals, arranged alternately with those already in place to make an outer layer. Bend the petals outwards.

Glue the calyx in position at the base of the flower, cupping the edges for a realistic effect.

Clematis

Flowers. Organza.
Petals. 5.5cm × 3cm, six per flower.
Bud. 3.5cm × 6cm, one per bud.
Centre. Inner layer: brown velvet or satin, 2.5cm × 3.5cm, one per flower.
Outer layer: organza as for petals, 1.5cm × 4.5cm, one per flower.
Leaves. 3.5cm × 2.5cm, two per flower.

How to work

Cut out the petals and leaves, and paint veins on the petals. Curl the petal edges with a heated knife handle and iron veins on to the leaves. Glue 24swg wires to the backs of the petals and to the leaves to support them.

Cut the velvet for the centre of the flowers into strips joined at their base. Wind and then glue a velveteen layer around a hook made of 18swg wire which has been hooked over the material at the base of the strips. Wind and glue the outer layer of organza around the inner velveteen layer so that the bases coincide but the inner layer projects above the outer.

Arrange six petals around the centre and fasten with 30swg wire and brown tape.

To make buds, glue a small ball of cotton wool over a hook of 24swg wire. Glue the bud petals over it by their edges to make a suitable shape.

An arrangement of clematis can look very effective when mixed with other fabric flowers (such as the russet-coloured poppies overleaf) and also with a few dried grasses.

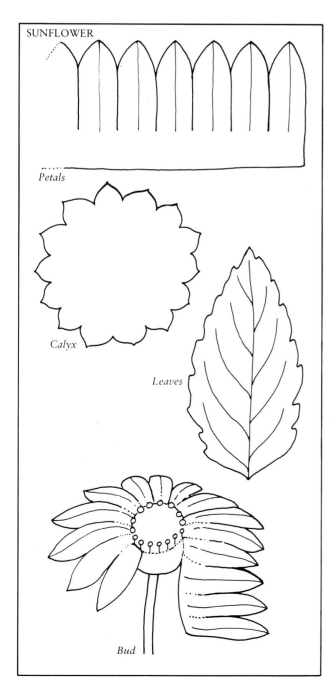

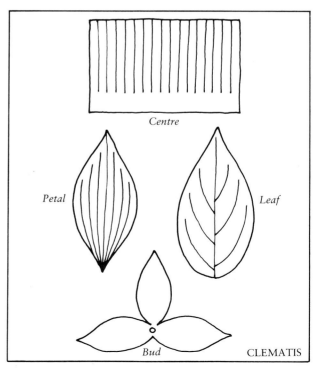

Autumn flowers. *Inspired by autumn, daffodils, clematis and poppies are made in fantasy tones of russet and sepia. The clematis is copied from a hybrid which has soft, rose-pink flowers but here it is made in burnt sienna to go with the other flowers.*

Snowdrops
(see picture page 9)

Flowers. White organza (silky) or silk.
Petals. Outer, 25cm × 25cm, one per flower; inner, 2cm × 2cm, one per flower.
Stamens. Orange material, 15cm × 1cm.
Leaves. Green cotton or satin, 8cm × 1cm.

How to work

Cut out all the petals and leaves. Paint the inner layer of petals green and mark the veins as in the diagram on

28

the opposite page, bottom. Pierce a hole in the centre of both petals, then curl the edges with a heated knife handle to form a cup shape.

To ensure that the stamens are central, cut the piece of orange material into small strips joined at their base. Bend a small hook of 24SWG green-covered wire, apply a little glue along the base, hook the wire over one end of the base between the strips and roll the material round the wire to form the centre. Cover the base of the centre with a narrow strip of green floral tape. Thread the wire through the hole in the disc of inner petals and secure to the centre with glue. Fasten the outer petals similarly. Cover the base in green tape to form the calyx. Bend the stalk forwards to make the flowers droop. Paint the leaves with a central white strip. Attach a 24SWG wire covered in green to the back of each leaf and fasten them to the stalk with green floral tape.

For clean results when working on a small scale, use only very small amounts of glue.

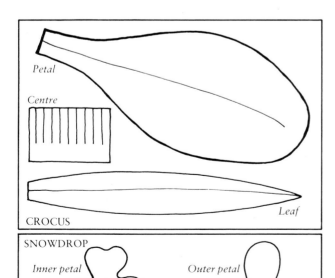

Crocus. *This bowl of mauve crocus shows how a little deft painting can enhance the appearance of flowers. Support wires are used on the petals to give the flowers their bell-like shape, while the stamens and orange anthers at the flower centres add a note of extra colour.*

Crocus

(see also picture, page 9)

Flowers. Organza (silky), silk or thin cotton, mauve, yellow or white.

Petals. 7.5cm × 3.5cm, six per flower.

Centre. 2.0cm × 1.5cm, one per flower (orange).

Leaves. Green cotton or satin, 8cm × 10cm, three per flower.

Stamens. Three, yellow, per flower.

How to work

Cut out the petals, mark the veins and shading on them. Curl the edges by ironing with a heated knife handle. Paint some 22SWG wire (covered in white) in the same colour as the petals and, when dry, glue it down the back of every petal as a support.

To make the centre, cut out the material and cut the top into small strips. Apply glue to the base, bend the end of a white-covered 24SWG wire into a small hook and insert it between the strips at one end. Roll this strip of material around itself. Cover the bottom with white tape to complete the pistil. Attach three yellow stamens 2cm below the top with white floral tape.

Join the petals on to the centre, three to make the inner layer and then, spaced between the inner petals, three to make the outer petals. Secure the petals with 30SWG wire covered with green floral tape. The closed crocus is bell-shaped.

Candelabra arrangement. *A glamorous display of orchids, roses, carnations and cherry blossom is held in place in a block of Plasticine which is covered in polythene film to protect the silver. A plastic candle-holder is stuck on top and the block is fastened to the centre of the candelabra with thin string.*

Cut out the leaves and paint a white stripe along the centre. Glue 24SWG green support wire on the back of each leaf and attach three leaves to each flower.

SHELL FLOWERS

SHELL FLOWERS

The variety of colour and quality, as well as their china appearance and beauty, all go to make shells an ideal medium with which to create flowers of all kinds.

Shells are not limited to one country. The search along the beaches of each new place visited and the seeking out of new shell shops adds even more interest to a pleasant pastime.

Usually, shells from the beach can be cleaned with luke-warm soapy water, but if they still contain their owners, put the shells in an old saucepan of water and bring it to the boil. This will kill the mollusc which can then be removed with a pin.

Storing shells can be a problem but plastic bags, boxes or discarded containers can be put to good use.

When working with shells, give yourself room to lay them out so that they can all be seen and be easily accessible. Give yourself plenty of room in which to work, too. If possible, find a room in which you can leave the items undisturbed until the glue, paste or plaster sets. This can often take 24 hours.

Most shell craft can be achieved by glueing. It is only in advanced work that shells need to be drilled or cut, so there is no complex or expensive equipment for the beginner to buy.

It is useful to know a little about the shells you collect, even though you are to use them purely for decoration. Buy or borrow a book and find out about them. Bivalves such as mussels are plentiful and they are useful as fillers. Other bivalves are cockles, which vary in colour from white to deep yellow, and tellins, which make splendid flowers and butterflies. Clams are similar to tellins and are excellent for petals. Univalves, such as periwinkles, are found in rock pools as are shiny cowries, long, pointed turritellas and spiralled whelks. Different names are often used for the same shell, so try to find out what your supplier calls each one. For instance, 'angels' wings' are piddocks, 'babies' fingernails' are tiny pink tellins, and 'tower shells' are turritellas.

As a useful reference, make a sampler of shells, mounting a specimen of each shell on cardboard, with its name and habitat printed underneath.

Collecting live shells

When collecting shells, take plastic bags, tissues and plastic boxes with you in which to put your more delicate finds, as they break very easily.

Some shells can be cut in half to show their attractive inner shapes, but you may find some damaged or water-worn shells which are just as interesting. If you do, gather these with the whole shells. This will both save time in cutting and add variety to your work.

Materials needed for shell flower-making

1. Green plastic-coated wire for stems (this can be doubled to hold heavier heads).
2. Fine wire, such as fuse or reel wire, for delicate work with seed heads and shell sprays.
3. Florists' tape, to cover the non-covered wires. This is usually available in green, natural and white colours.
4. Clear glue and fast-drying glue. Apply with a cocktail stick or a match stick on small areas, and with a glue spreader on larger ones. Many varieties of glue are obtainable.
5. Buttons, for shell flower mounts. They are easily obtainable and strong enough to stand the weight of the shells and the wire stem. They also have the advantage of having ready-drilled holes. Colour is not very important as the button is usually covered by the shells, but green is always a good choice.
6. Tweezers, for picking up small shells and for re-arranging them while working.
7. Empty jam jars.
8. Paper tissues to put over the tops of jars to support shells while the glue dries. Also useful for making buds and seed heads (as is cotton wool).
9. Plastic foam, for corn heads and for arranging flowers. Harder than 'Oasis', it is less liable to crumble.
10. Scissors, for cutting florists' tape and wire cutters for cutting wires.
11. A large variety of shells. The more shells you have, the greater the variety of flowers you will be able to produce.

How to make a simple shell flower

1. Cut as many lengths of green wire as there are to be flowers. Vary the lengths (30cm is about the average length for a flower stem).

This picture shows a mixture of shells from all over the world, including British cockles, and periwinkles, African snakes-head dowries, littorines, dentilla and rose petals, and others from the Caribbean.

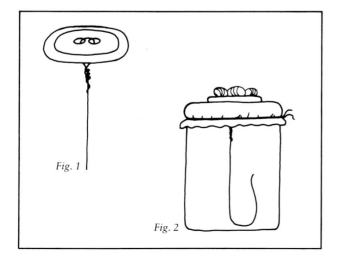

Fig. 1

Fig. 2

2. Attach the wire to the button by threading it through the holes and twisting the short end tightly around the longer end immediately below the button (Fig. 1).

3. Balance the button on a tissue, held taut over a jar or bowl with an elastic band. Insert the stem through the tissue, bending up the wire if necessary (Fig. 2).

4. Apply adhesive to the surface of the button and carefully arrange four or five shells around it so that the shells just touch in petal-like formation. Glue a small top shell or periwinkle in the centre.

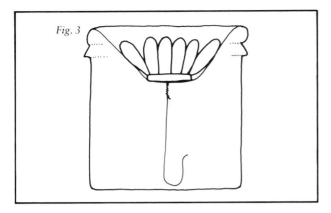

Fig. 3

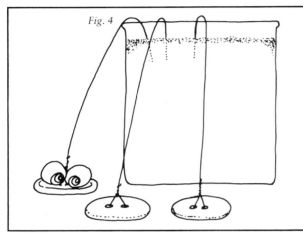

Fig. 4

5. Cup the petals of the flower, hollow out the tissue and rest the button at the bottom of the hollow. The sides of the tissue will support the shells. The tightness of the cup depends on the depth of the hollow and in this way you can vary the shape of each flower (Fig. 3).

This basic method of flower-making can be applied to the following shells: slipper limpets, mussels, tellins, wedge shells and piddocks, but shells should all be the same size. With some shells, care should be taken to note in which direction the shells face and to match them evenly.

Many shells have more colour or pattern on one side than the other, so choose the more attractive side to be uppermost.

An alternative method of attaching shells to buttons is to glue them to the back of a button. Place the button face down on the table and support the stems in a jar of sand (Fig. 4). This is a good way to start when multiple layers of shells are to be used or if the button is attractive enough to be used as the centre. Do not disturb the shells until the glue is completely dry.

Varieties

Here are some suggestions for varieties of flowers, based on the foregoing instructions.

Rose: use graded tellins, starting with the outer and bigger shells at the back of the button and building up gradually to the centre at the front of the button. If the glue is slow to dry, support the inner shells with little rolls of tissue paper. White cockles work just as well and you can mix pink and white shells.

Daisies: long white piddocks (angels' wings) glued to the front of buttons with yellow periwinkle centres make fine daisies.

Pansies or violas: large wedge shells or purple butterfly clams make excellent pansies or violas. Their colours vary from deep purple to pink or white. Only three are needed per flower, so choose two which face in opposite directions and another of the same size. Glue them to the face of the button with the pair at the top, the other below and a small shell in the centre.

For a different centre, a lot of little tellins, topshells or yellow periwinkles can be massed in the middle of larger, contrasting shells.

When wiring buttons, add a few stamens, which can be threaded through the button holes.

When a flower is finished, cut a strip of green crepe paper into five points to make a calyx. Place it close under the button and bind it in place with florists' tape. A touch of glue at the back of the button will help to keep it in place.

Many additional types of flower and seed heads can be made, occasionally with damaged shells. Grasses can be made from Dog whelks and leaf sprays from cockles or mussels. Use the holes to wire several shells with thin reel wire, then bind together in spray formation and bind on to a thicker stem wire.

Use black periwinkles to make sprays of blackberries. Secure cotton wool buds to a loop of reel wire, coat it with glue and push it deep into the shell. Bind the individual shells on to a stronger wire with the smallest shells at the tip, graduating to the largest at the bottom. Cover all the thin wires with florists' tape cut in half.

Another group of flowers, such as Pink May or Sweet William, can be formed by making several tiny heads in the usual way on fine wires, then binding them together at one point on to a stronger stem. Cover the wire ends with florists' tape.

Larger single cornlike heads or buds can be made by binding small pieces of foam with wire, coating them in glue and laying the shells carefully on to them. Do one half at a time, working from the top and overlapping each·a little. Use long tapering pieces of foam and narrow shells for corn, with round ones and cockles for the buds.

Always make plenty of flowers, about four or five of each kind, as you need plenty to fill a vase. Even if you do not use them all, the left-over ones will come in useful for another time.

Make bell-like flowers by sticking together two cup-shaped shells, one tucked into the other so that they

A beautiful arrangement of shell flowers, using the simplest and most common of shells such as tellins, periwinkles and cockles. The flowers are enhanced by dried leaves which add softness and contrast.

form a bell. Stick a wired bell cap on the base of the shells and bind each flower head on to a thin wire, attached to a central branch so that they hang like bells.

Perhaps the easiest flowers of all to make are 'butter-fly' flowers. These are simply two scallop shells stuck together back to back, with a small shell stuck

between them. Add a tiny bead to the centre. Stick on to a wired button and bind in an artificial leaf.

Many flowers can be made more realistic by adding small extra touches. For instance, when wiring buttons, thread some stamens (obtainable from craft shops) through them. A few leaves add greatly to the charm of a shell flower arrangement. These can be silk ones, or dried, or you can make some by cutting strips of green crepe paper into five points, then placing them close under the button of the finished flower and binding them in place with florists' tape or narrow strips of paper. A touch of glue will hold the leaves in place.

Another colourful arrangement of shell flowers, this time in a basket. Again, they are complemented by a few dried leaves. The shells used are slightly different from those in the picture on the opposite page, but none are hard to find.

Containers for flowers

When choosing containers for arrangements, a lot will depend on what you have in the house, but do not forget that shells, if large enough, make decorative containers in themselves.

A block of driftwood, with foam glued to it, will also serve well as a container base for an arrangement.

Dried flowers

To make an arrangement more attractive and natural-looking, do not hesitate to use dried and pressed leaves. Even hedgerow plants such as Old Man's Beard, thistles or twigs can be included.

Dried flowers and seed heads can be used to great advantage in shell flower-making. Use them instead of buttons on which to mount shells and you will have some very unusual flowers. Ideal dried flowers for this purpose are poppy seed heads, achillea, cotton grass and campion, all of which can be used with any combination of shells. However, do remember that the stems will be too brittle to bend, and that

Blue muscle shells which vary from deep blue to these lighter striped ones are very common. They make effective flowers either with periwinkles or dried achilles as their centres.

such flowers will either have to have their heads placed on wires or be used as a small part of an arrangement where their stiffness will not be too noticeable.

Sand and polished pebbles can also be used in shell flower arrangements to add interest and colour.

Arranging shell flowers

When arranging shell flowers, it is a good idea to decide right from the start the shape you wish to

37

achieve. Begin with your outline, either fan-shaped or sweeping from right to left or left to right, depending on where it is to be placed.

Usually the lighter weights and lighter coloured flowers or sprays go at the outer edge, gradually working inwards towards the heavier sizes and colours nearer the centre and towards the bottom. This will give a balanced and natural look, with all the stems and sprays directed towards one focal point.

In a free-standing arrangement a slight backward lean will help with the weight and prevent the flowers from looking as though they are falling forward. Sometimes a weight is needed in the bowl to help balance the heavier heads.

How to make a shell flower picture

You will need:
A large assortment of shells;
A piece of hardboard;
Paint or fabric to cover the hardboard;
A recessed frame to fit, with glass for it;
Clear and epoxy adhesives.

A fine everlasting wedding bouquet in shades of pink and white 'roses' made from white cockles, tiny pink tellins ('baby's fingernails') and pearly top shells with a delicate background of tusk shell sprays, white goose feathers and pink satin ribbons.

Prepare the board by colouring or covering it. Make up some flowers separately, using rounded shells for petals, small shells for sprays etc. Make plenty of flowers, as a skimpy arrangement will not look attractive. See in the illustration (opposite) how varied the flowers are. This variety of shape and form helps to make a picture lively. Note too how different shades and colours are mixed and contrasted, and how some shells are used on their own to add still more variety.

Make a few rough sketches, before you begin, of the kind of picture you have in mind, bearing in mind the sort of shells you have to work with. You can do a trial arrangement on a piece of board, then transfer it later. Do not draw on the mounting board because marks are very difficult to remove.

When you are pleased with your trial run and you have made enough flowers, stick them in place, using

clear or epoxy adhesive, depending on the weight of the flowers. Frame under glass.

Another way of making a simple shell picture is to set them in wet plaster of Paris, in a shallow wooden tray which can then be framed behind glass. When

A striking shell flower picture in which many of the flowers are whole shells. Small pieces of white coral make a striking contrast to the black background, and the subtle colours of the yellow and orange periwinkles complement those of the larger shells. The fern-like flowers are made from white tusk shells.

Bright red coral branches enliven this tiny shell flower arrangement set in a wooden egg cup and composed of tusk shells, tellins and top shells. The small silver shells are 'venetians', particularly useful for flower making.

(Page 41)

Cockle shells and rose cups are the basis of most of the flowers in this candlestick arrangement. The shape of the flowers is greatly enhanced and softened by the use of dried leaves. A piece of 'Oasis' is essential to hold together a group of this kind.

setting shells in cement of any kind you must plan your picture beforehand. Try out the design on a piece of material. The design can be like a mosaic, with the stronger colour and shapes standing out against a background filled with plain shells, or it can be a simple arrangement of shells against a plaster background. Once the design is decided, transfer it to the wet plaster in the tray and let it set.

40

Shell boxes

Keep your shells in boxes and decorate them with shells! Wooden boxes are best for this. Make a practice design on a board first, to make sure you have enough shells to cover the whole box. Sandpaper the box until you have a smooth surface, then, working on one side of the box at a time, cover it with glue or a layer of filler, and starting from the centre, work your design.

A light coat of varnish when the box is finished will bring out the colours. Leave a space along the hinged edge, or the shells will shatter when the box is opened.

This unusual arrangement, using an antique tea caddy, displays flowers of slipper limpets with a large central flower of trough shells. The finer sprays of buds are made from dog whelks and the whole is set off against dried leaves and driftwood.

(Page 43)

This elaborate arrangement makes use of a Victorian glass dome and part of its original contents. The oasis in which the shell flowers, driftwood and dried flowers are arranged is disguised with dried moss and lichen placed to look as natural as possible. The shell flowers are of cockles and periwinkles with a few sprays of baby pink tellins.

A wide range of shells is used in these arrangements.
Left, top: *cockles and periwinkles predominate in the
large flowers, with the cockles repeated in the sprays
of buds. Tusk shells form the more delicate flowers
with sprays of dog whelks and coral giving the final
touches to the background.*

Left, bottom: *mauve tellins form the petals of these
flowers, grouped effectively in a large shell with some
honesty seed heads.*

Above: *with driftwood as a firm base, white daisies,
'angel's wings' or piddocks, are set off by dried
grasses, while dried tassels of love-lies-bleeding are
arranged in 'oasis' glued to the driftwood.*

This autumnal arrangement is of tusk shell daisies with brown and yellow periwinkle centres also mounted on driftwood. The flowers are set against and complemented by the brown and biscuit colours of the dried grasses and pheasant feathers.

46

BREAD-DOUGH FLOWERS

BREAD-DOUGH FLOWERS

Bread dough sculpture is an ancient craft practised in Mexico from many centuries ago. It is believed to have been originated by women who wanted to make ornaments and jewelry with the readily available materials which could be found about the home.

The recipe given below has substituted some modern materials, such as white PVA glue and acrylic paint, but otherwise the basic bread recipe remains much the same.

When the ingredients have been mixed together, the resulting substance resembles a sort of Plasticine, which can be kept in a polythene bag in a plastic container in the refrigerator. Small amounts can be used as required and the mixture will keep like this and be usable for six to ten weeks.

Working with bread dough is rather like modelling with Plasticine, except that each modelled part is attached with a small spot of glue. When the mixture dries it becomes hard and when painted and glazed it resembles bone china.

Materials and equipment

113g white bread
3 level tablespoonsful of white glue
1 level tablespoonful white acrylic paint
1 level teaspoon glycerine
3 drops lemon juice
Flower wires
Green florists' tape
Reel wire
Clay modelling tools (or tools from a manicure set)
Nail scissors

Mixing the dough

1. Take four slices of white bread from a medium thick sliced loaf. Use bread about two days old but if the bread is very fresh and moist, leave it out for an hour or so until it becomes firm but not dry. Remove crusts from bread and pull the bread into small pieces. Weigh the bread to make sure there is a full 113g. Place the bread in a medium-sized mixing bowl.
2. Carefully measure all the other ingredients into the bowl with the bread. Accuracy is very important. It is better to under-measure the liquid ingredients than to over-measure them.
3. Mix the ingredients with a spoon. When the mixture begins to hold together and gradually comes away from the sides of the bowl, remove it and knead the dough in the palms of the hands. (Remember to soak the bowl in water immediately after mixing to remove the acrylic paint.) Continue to knead the mixture by squeezing it in the palms of the hands and passing it from one hand to the other. At this stage the mixture will begin to dry out. As the mixture dries it improves in texture and should start to pull away from the hands, leaving them clean and free from dough.

The kneading process takes about 20 minutes and requires a little patience. Sometimes, if the water content in the bread is high, the dough remains rather sticky. In this case, and if after kneading for 20 minutes the mixture has not reached the right consistency, add a little more bread (a half or one slice) and knead this in until modelling consistency is reached.
4. To store the mixture, put it in the corner of a plastic bag. Remove as much air from the bag as possible and seal it. Place it in a plastic container and store in the refrigerator until required.

Pre-modelling tips

1. Never remove from the bag more dough than you need at a time, as it hardens fairly quickly. If the dough becomes too hard during modelling, knead a few drops of water into it.

When the dough comes out of the refrigerator it will be quite cold and hard, so knead the dough you are to use to make it pliable.
2. All flower wires must be covered with floral tape to prevent rusting.
3. Always dry flowers at normal room temperature.
4. Always glaze flowers in a dry atmosphere.
5. A glue bottle with a dispenser is a useful device for applying small drops of glue but if you do not have one, place glue in a saucer and apply it with a match stick.
6. Only white glue is used throughout. It forms a strong bond if left undisturbed for several hours to dry.
7. When drying flowers, most can be supported on crumpled tissue paper but very large flowers are best

supported in the neck of a wine bottle. Many flowers can be stood on their heads to dry, the wire pointing upwards. Find the most suitable drying method for each flower you make.

8. Push flower wires into a piece of polystyrene foam while modelling, then you will not have to lay them down on the table. Polystyrene will also support flower centres while they dry.

9. Thin the edges of petals and leaves after modelling by gently pressing the edges between finger and thumb.

10. Use reference books or seed catalogues as a guide to making and colouring.

11. Use handcream to prevent dough sticking to the hands while you are working.

Colouring the dough

Tubes of watercolour paint and egg tempera or tempera paints are excellent for colouring. Break off a piece of dough the size of a walnut. Flatten it and add a little colour from the tube to the dough. Keep folding the dough over and kneading it to distribute the colour evenly. Experiment to find the depth of colour required. If the colour becomes too intense, add more white dough. Paint acts as a preservative, so coloured dough keeps longer than white dough.

Painting bread dough flowers

Most paints are suitable for painting finished models. Oil paints can be used but they take a long time to dry, so poster colours, acrylics, temperas and water-colours are most successful. Watercolours give a lovely, soft translucent look to finished models.

Covering flower wires

Cut a piece of green floral tape. Stretch it to its full extent. Take a flower wire and cover the tip with the tape. Holding the tape-covered wire between the first finger and thumb of one hand and, holding the tape taut with the other hand, spin the wire between finger and thumb, spiralling the tape down and along the wire to cover it. (Diagrams 35 and 36 on page 66.)

Glazing

Plastic glaze can be bought in craft shops for glazing finished models. The most commonly used one (DAS) gives a high gloss finish that resembles a bone china glaze. You can also buy a spray which gives a matt finish and a look of real porcelain. Nail lacquers can also be used both for colouring and as a clear glaze.

An easy and inexpensive glaze can be made by mixing a 50/50 solution of water and white glue. Coat the models three times with this, leaving them to dry between each coat. This glaze will prevent cracking, especially on larger models, and a very high gloss can be obtained if they are baked for 3–5 minutes in an oven at a temperature of 250°C.

Make sure that all models are dried out before glazing.

This bowl of carefully modelled flowers includes roses, bluebells, marsh marigolds and narcissi. Each petal is separately modelled and then all are glued together.

Flowers modelled on to dried materials

This is an excellent way of producing a flower arrangement quickly, as the stems and leaves are already provided. Flowers look pretty and realistic modelled on to green dried Ruscus, and the red dried Ruscus looks attractive too, although it also looks more artificial.

1. Take a Ruscus or similar type of spray and remove the leaf at the top of each stem.

2. Take a piece of dough the size of a pea. Place a small amount of glue on the tip of the stem, where the leaf was removed and press the dough flower centre on to the tip of the stem.

3. Supporting the flower centre between finger and thumb press a tea strainer down on to the flower centre, to leave an attractive squared impression.

4. Leave to dry for six hours.

5. Take five more small pieces of dough the size of small peas. Press them flat to make into petal shapes and pinch them at the edge to form a stem on the petal.

6. Place a small spot of glue on each petal stem and attach each petal individually round the flower centre. Press well into position.

An enchanting bouquet of bread dough flowers that includes tulips, buttercups and roses. The dough can be coloured before modelling and detail can be added later. A glaze is added to give a porcelain-like finish.

This close-up of bread dough flowers shows their fine porcelain-like finish.

7. Pinch the centre of the outer edge of the petals to add shape. Gently bend the petals upwards and inwards.

8. Leave them to dry. Then paint and glaze.

How to make bread dough roses

1. Take a piece of dough the size of a large pea. Roll it into a worm shape and flatten it to form an oval, pointed at both ends (see Diagram 1).

Place a small amount of glue along one of the long straight edges and roll it into a coil.

Dip the tip of a flower wire into glue and push it well into the centre of the coil. Pinch well at the base to secure it to the wire (Diagram 2). Leave to dry for six hours standing in a piece of polystyrene foam.

Diagram 1

Diagram 3

Diagram 2

Diagram 4a

Diagram 4b

Diagram 5a

Instructions for making a spray of yellow roses like these are given on this and the opposite page.

2. Take three small pieces of dough the size of small peas and flatten them to form small circles (Diagram 3). Thin the edges of the dough between finger and thumb. Put a small spot of glue at the outer edge of each circle and attach each one separately to the flower centre, slightly overlapping each petal.

3. Make four more small rose petals and attach them to the rose in the same way.

4. Make five more petals but make them a little larger and slightly more oval-shaped than the previous four. Attach these petals behind the last row of petals, spacing them evenly round the outer edge.

5. When the rose is complete, curl the edges of some of the rose petals by gently pressing the petals downwards along the outer edges.

Calyx

1. Take a small piece of green dough, shape it into a triangle and flatten it.

2. Cut one edge into five V-shapes as shown in Diagram 4a.

3. Place a small amount of glue at the base of the flower and also along one of the straight edges of the calyx. Attach the calyx to cover the base of the flower and the upper part of the stem.

4. Bend the tips of the calyx outwards and downwards from the flower (Diagram 4b).

Rose leaves

Leaves are usually made and fastened to thin reel wire but they can be attached directly to the flower stem wire. The easiest way to make a leaf is to press the dough on to a plastic leaf, or even a real leaf. This gives

a beautiful clear impression complete with veining. Always use this method for the veining even if the leaf is modelled by hand, as it will save a lot of time. The following instructions for making leaves and a leaf spray can be used for most types of leaves.

Leaf spray

1. Take a small piece of green dough and press it down on to a plastic or real leaf. Peel the dough impression away from the leaf. Trim and serrate the edges of the leaf with nail scissors, either by cutting or by pressing the tip of the scissors into the edge of the leaf.
2. Take a piece of green-covered reel wire and glue the tip of the wire. Press 5mm of the wire down on to the lower part of the leaf. Pinch the base of the leaf to secure and conceal the wire (Diagram 5a).

A bouquet of easily recognisable Dog roses, their petals delicately shaded from dark to light pink. Real leaves are mixed with the bread dough leaves.

3. Make two more, slightly smaller, leaves in the same way. Tape each individual leaf on to its own short length of reel wire. Attach these two smaller leaves to the main wire close to the stem with floral tape. Rose leaf sprays are usually in groups of 3, 5 or 7. Another pair of leaves can be attached if desired.

Rose bud

To make a rose bud, carry out steps 1 and 2 for the rose, and attach a calyx.

53

Dog rose

Flower centre

1. Roll a piece of yellow dough into a ball to make the flower centre and push it through a small square of nylon net (or a nylon stocking for finer detail) cut to approximately 4cm square. Gather the material together at the base and pinch it well to maintain a ball shape.
2. Glue the end of the flower wire and push this into the base of the flower centre.
3. Leave to dry for about six hours and, when dry, carefully cut or gently pull away the net material from the outer edge. (Diagram 5b.)

Petals

1. Take a piece of pink dough the size of a small pea. Mould between the fingers into a triangular shape and flatten.
2. With nail scissors, round off two corners and cut away a small V-shape at the centre between the two rounded edges. This gives a heart-shaped petal. Thin the outside edges between the fingers. Make five more petals like this.
3. Place a small amount of glue on to the pointed end of each petal. Attach the petals evenly spaced around the base of the flower centre. Gently bend some of the petal edges upwards and inwards for added effect.
4. Make and attach a calyx and leaves as for the rose.

Diagram 5b

Diagram 6a

Marsh Marigold

Flower centre

Make a flower centre as for the Dog rose (Diagram 5b) and leave to dry for six hours.

Petals

1. Break off five small pieces of yellow-coloured dough. Roll into small balls and flatten into slightly oval-shaped petals.
2. Cup one hand and place a petal in the centre of the palm of the cupped hand. With the rounded end of a modelling tool, gently stroke the centre of the petal. Continue with this action until a cup-shaped appearance develops. Cup each of the remaining petals like this.
3. Place a spot of glue at the base of each oval petal shape and press them into position at the base of the flower centre. Petals should be slightly overlapped.

Leaves

Flatten a piece of green dough and cut it into a leaf shape as in Diagram 6a. Leaves should be twice the size of a flower head. Attach a flower wire to the base of the leaf by glueing.

Primrose

Flower centre

1. Take a very small piece of yellow dough to make a flower centre (about four flower centres can be made from a piece of dough the size of a pea).
2. Glue to the tip of a flower wire and push the wire into the base of the small, ball-shaped flower centre.
3. Gently pinch the top of the flower centre to form a dome-shaped top and leave to dry for six hours.

Flower Petals

1. Take a piece of dough the size of a very large pea. Press this into a flat circular shape.
2. Using small nail scissors, divide the dough into five equal sections by cutting into the edges. Take care not to cut too deeply into the centre as the petal sections must remain intact (Diagram 6b).
3. Shape each of these individual petals by cutting the outside edges into a heart shape (Diagram 7).
4. Thin the outer edges of petals by pressing between the fingers.

A basket of delicate yellow marsh marigolds is set off to perfection on real stems with dark green dried leaves. The textured flower centres are made by pressing dough into nylon net.

Natural looking primroses look well in a brass vase, with plenty of leaves. When possible, take an impression of real leaves in the dough, as this makes them look more realistic.

Leaves

If possible, make leaves with an impression taken from a real primrose or polyanthus.

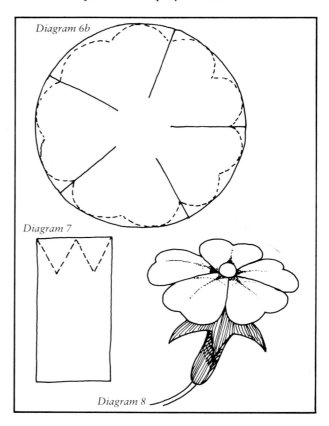

5. Make a deep impression line along the centre of each petal by pressing with the modelling tool.
6. Glue the base of the flower centre. Attach flower to the flower centre by pushing the wire through the centre of the circle of petals. Press well into position.

Calyx

Press a piece of green dough into a rectangular shape about 1cm × 2cm. Cut one of the shorter edges into three pointed sections (Diagram 8).

Place glue along the straight edge of the calyx and also at the base of the flower. Wrap the calyx around the wire just below the base of the flower until the calyx is edge to edge. Press into position, making sure the calyx is stuck to the base of the flower. Make lines with scissors lengthways along the calyx to give a grooved appearance. Bend the cut edges of the calyx downwards.

Bluebells

Stamens

1. Mould and flatten a small piece of yellow dough into a rectangular shape just over 1cm × ½cm.
2. Fringe the shortest edge very finely about three quarters of the way along the strip (Diagram 9, 10).
3. Glue a piece of covered reel wire about ½cm from the end of the wire.

Bell-shaped flowers

1. Take a small piece of blue dough and roll it into a cone shape.
2. Press and hollow out the centre of the shape with a modelling tool to make a bell shape.
3. Make lines around the outside of the bell by pressing with scissors.
4. Make small cuts around the outer edge of the bell and press the edges to curl outwards (Diagram 11).
5. Lightly glue the base of the flower centre and push the reel wire through the cupped bell shape to secure.
6. Make several of these flowers for each stem.

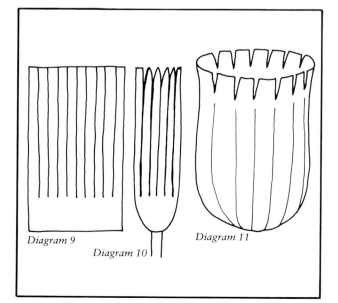

Top: *a spray of bluebells and a spray of roses, made of separate flowers joined with tape.* Bottom: *a group of dark pansies on a ribbon makes an unusual bookmark.*

7. Place one bell on a long piece of reel wire and fasten more bells one below the other at regular intervals, joining the wires together with floral tape.

Leaves

1. Roll a piece of green dough into a worm shape 6cm−7½cm long, about ½cm diameter. Press it into a long flat shape.
2. Trim both ends to a point. With scissors or modelling tool, make vein lines along the length of the leaf.
3. Glue reel wire 2½cm longer than the leaf along the centre back of the leaf.
4. Make several leaves like this. Bend and twist some.
5. Leave to dry, and add a touch of green paint to give depth of colour. Wire to the main stem or use separately.

Diagram 9

Diagram 10

Diagram 11

Narcissi

Narcissi can look very pretty arranged around the base of a catkin tree or in a miniature plant pot. The cap from a large shampoo bottle or similar container makes a useful pot for a single flower.

Stamens and flower centre

1. Take a piece of yellow dough and roll it between the fingers into as thin a strip as possible. Cut this strip into sections 1¼cm long.
2. Make six thin strips and pinch the tip of each one to flatten it.
3. Glue these round a flower wire to make the flower centre. Leave to dry.
4. Take a very small, pea-sized piece of orange dough and roll it into a cone shape.
5. Make a hollow in the centre of the cone shape by pressing it with a pointed modelling tool. Thin the edges of the dough as much as possible.
6. Using the blade of the scissors, make indentations on the inside edge of the cone centre and also make a few tiny cuts along the outer edge at irregular intervals (Diagram 12).
7. Place a small amount of glue at the base of the stamens and push the flower wire through the centre of the cone. Leave to dry for six hours (Diagram 13).

Petals

1. Take a piece of white dough and press it into a flat circular shape about 3cm in diameter.
2. Divide the circle into six equal sections, letting these sections remain intact at the centre. To do this, make two cuts from the outer edge into the circle of dough. These cuts must be directly opposite each other. Make two more cuts in each semi-circle to give three sections in each half and making six equal sections altogether in the circle (Diagram 14).
3. Shape the petals by cutting away the pointed area at the outer edges of the dough petal shapes (Diagram 15).
4. Make indentations along the centre of each petal with the blade of the scissors.
5. Pinch the centre edge of the petals to add shape and bend the petal edges slightly inwards.
6. Glue the base of the flower centre and push through the circle of petals.
7. When dry, gently bend the head of the flower over until it is at right angles to the flower wire.

To make leaves, follow the directions for the crocus leaves on page 60. Paint the flower centre yellow or orange. The cup-shaped cone looks very pretty painted yellow with orange edges. The petals remain white.

Anemones

Flower centre

1. Take a small piece of black dough the size of a pea. Glue the top of the flower wire. Press the dough into position on top of the flower wire.
2. Take a nylon mesh tea-strainer and press it well down on to the flower centre to leave a square design impression on the flower centre. This is quick and easy to do (Diagram 16).
3. Make a fringe from the dough as for the Christmas rose flower centre (page 64) and attach it round the outer edge of the flower centre.
4. Leave to dry for six hours.

Petals

1. Take eight pieces of dough the size of small peas. Roll each piece into a tear shape and press them flat (Diagram 17).

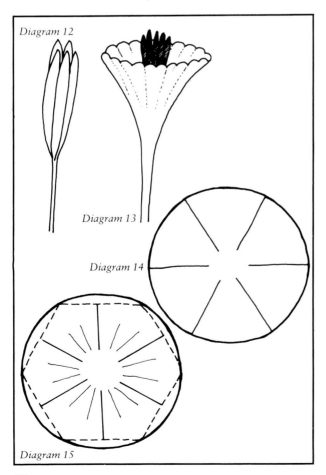

Diagram 12

Diagram 13

Diagram 14

Diagram 15

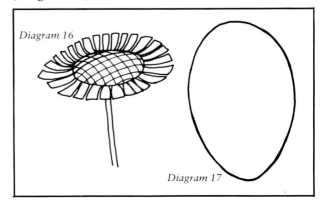

Diagram 16

Diagram 17

2. Add a spot of glue to the pointed base of four of the petals and attach them to the base of the flower centre, making sure each one is evenly spaced. Attach the remaining four petals and place alternately behind the first four petals.

3. Gently bend and curl the petal edges upwards and slightly inwards.

Anemones can be shaded in blues, pinks, red, lavender and white. Refer to seed catalogues for colour ideas.

Looking like a lovely underwater plant, this arrangement of blue, red, pink and white anemones is softened by the starry white dried flowers. These, though bearing no resemblance to real anemone leaves, add variety to the shapes. The porcelain-like finish on the bread dough flowers is clearly seen in this picture.

59

A close-up of the anemones on the previous page. Note how the flowers have been carefully painted to imitate closely the natural colours of the red anemone. When making any flowers, it is always best to refer to good photographs or, better still, to model directly from nature when possible.

Crocus

Stamens

1. Take a piece of orange dough and roll it between the palms of the hands or fingers into a very thin strip about the thickness of a darning needle.
2. Break off three pieces 2cm long. Glue these in place 1¼cm in from the end of a flower wire. Flatten the tips of the stamens between the fingers.
3. Take a very small piece of dough and roll it into a pellet shape. Add a small amount of glue around the base of the stamens and attach the pellet-shaped piece of dough round the base. Press well into position and leave to dry for six hours (Diagram 18).

Flower petals

1. Break off six pieces of white dough, each the size of a pea. Press into oval-shaped petals. At one end pinch between the fingers to form a short stem. Lay the petal on the cupped palm of one hand and gently stroke the centre area of the petal with the rounded end of a modelling tool until it curls and forms a cup shape (Diagram 19).
2. Place a small amount of glue on the short stem of each petal. Attach three of the crocus petals evenly spaced round the flower centre. Attach the three remaining petals, spacing them alternately behind the first three petals.

Leaves

1. Roll a piece of green dough into a 'worm' shape 6cm–7½cm long, and about ½cm in diameter. Press into a long flat shape.
2. Trim both ends to a point. With scissors or a modelling tool, make vein lines along the length of the leaf. (Diagrams 20, 21, 22.)
3. Glue a piece of reel wire 2½cm longer than the leaf along the centre back of the leaf.
4. Make several leaves in this way. Bend and twist some for more realism.
5. Leave to dry in the usual way. Even though green dough is used, a touch of green paint adds greater depth of colour to the leaf. Leaves can be wired into the main flower stem or used separately.

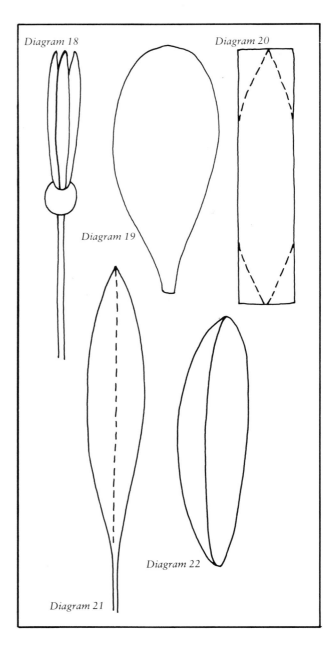

Diagram 18

Diagram 19

Diagram 20

Diagram 21

Diagram 22

Two or three lovely water lilies like this would make a superb table decoration. The broad green leaves set off the yellow- centred symmetrical petals to perfection.

Water-lily

Flower centre

1. Take a ball of yellow dough and flatten the top.
2. With a modelling tool mark the flat top surface of the flower centre into eight sections. Glue the flower centre on to the top of the flower wire in the usual way.
3. Take another piece of yellow dough. Roll it into a 'worm' shape, press flat and fringe finely one of the long edges of the dough.
4. Glue the straight edge and attach this to the outer edge of the flower centre.
5. Make another strip and attach in the same way. Gently curve the fringes outwards by pressing with the fingers. Leave to dry. (Diagram 23.)

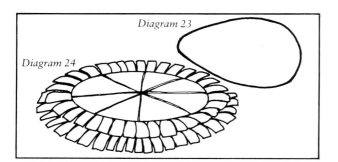

Diagram 23

Diagram 24

Petals

1. Take a piece of white dough the size of a very small pea. Mould it into a tear shape and press flat.
2. Place a small amount of glue on to the rounded end of the petal and attach just below the flower centre. Continue to make enough petals to complete the first circle of petals which should be evenly spaced round the flower centre. Normally about seven petals are needed. (Diagram 24.)
3. Add another row of petals.
4. Pinch the tips of the petals on these first two rows. This cups the petals slightly and helps them to stand up round the flower centre.
5. Make enough petals to add three more rows of petals to the water-lily. Remember to make the third and fourth rows of petals slightly larger as the flower gets bigger. Leave to dry.
6. Remove the flower wire by cutting it away as close to the base as possible.

Leaves

1. Take a piece of green dough the size of a hazel nut, roll it into a ball and press flat.
2. Make a cut in the circle a quarter of the way in from the outer edge.
3. Trim the outer edge to give a slightly uneven appearance.
4. Give the leaf shape an added interest by dividing the top into six sections. Do this by pinching the surface of the dough between the fingers to form slight ridges from the outer edges and towards the centre. This larger leaf should be about the size of the water-lily flower itself.
5. Make another leaf slightly smaller than this and a third leaf about half the size of the largest leaf.
6. Paint a deep leaf green. Use fairly thick paint as this gives an interesting two-tone effect to the leaf.
7. Glaze when dry.
8. Glue into position by interlocking the leaves and the cut edges. Glue the water-lily on top of the leaves.

Magnolia tree

Select an interesting tree-shaped branch from a tree on which to attach the blossoms. These are made separately, then individually stuck to the twig or branch. Make the blossoms directly on to a flower wire as usual, then cut the wire away as close as possible to the flower before fastening to the tree.

Flower centre

1. Take a piece of yellow dough the size of a very small pea and roll this into an elongated bud shape.
2. Place a small amount of glue on the tip of the flower wire and press the wider end of the flower centre on to the flower wire.

3. Take a pin and prick the flower centre all over to make lots of small indentations. (Diagram 25.)

4. Flatten a small piece of yellow dough into a narrow oblong shape about 1¼cm deep. Fringe this closely with nail scissors.

5. Place glue along the uncut edge and attach this below the flower centre. (Diagram 26.) Leave to dry.

Petals

1. Take five white pieces of dough each the size of a small pea. Press flat and make into oval petal shapes. (Diagram 27.) Pinch one end slightly to narrow it and give a pear-shaped appearance to the petal. Hollow and curve the petal centre as for the crocus petals on page 60.

2. Place glue on the narrow end of the petal and attach each one round the flower centre. Arrange the petals so that they seem to be open and therefore in full bloom. Leave to dry for six hours.

3. When dry, remove the flower wire as close to the base of the flower as possible. Use pliers if necessary.

Calyx

1. Take four very small pieces of green dough to form into leaf shapes for the calyx. (These pieces should be about one third the size of the petals.) (Diagram 28.)

2. Roll dough into tiny bud shapes. Flatten the dough to form tiny leaves. Glue these into position around the base of the flower blossoms. Leave to dry.

Painting and glazing

Blossoms can be left white or be painted an ivory colour. Blend in traces of pink at the centre and the base of the petals to give a realistic look. Glazing can be carried out before attaching the blossoms to the tree or afterwards.

Attaching the blossoms

Take a tiny ball of green dough and glue this to the base of the flower blossom where the calyx leaves meet.

Add more glue to the small ball of dough and press into position on to a branch from a tree.

Usually blossoms stay put quite well while the glue is setting, but if any trouble is experienced a strip of white tissue paper can be gently wound round the blossom and the branch to which the blossom is attached. This will help to hold it in position until the glue sets, then it can be removed.

Make leaves as per Diagram 29.

Press the finished Magnolia tree into Plasticine or a bread dough mixture. Cover the base with moss or dried material (obtainable from florists). The branch can be preserved by painting it with one or two coats of a 50/50 solution of water and white glue.

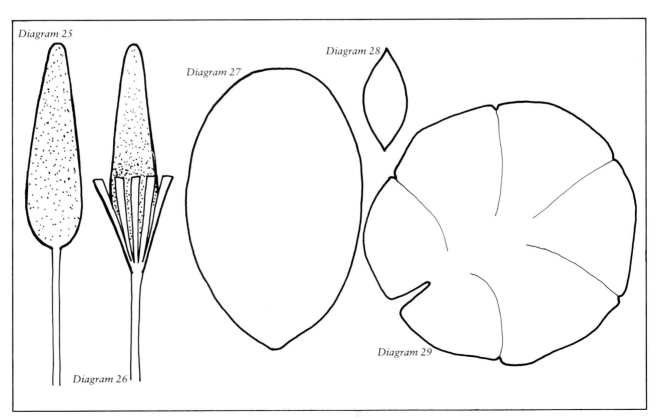

Diagram 25

Diagram 27

Diagram 28

Diagram 26

Diagram 29

Pansies

Flower centre

Take a very small piece of yellow dough. Roll into a ball and glue into position on the end of a flower wire. Leave to dry for six hours. (Diagram 30, overleaf.)

Flower petals

1. Take five pieces of yellow dough, size of small peas.
2. Press each one of these shapes flat to make petals. Thin one of the petals a little more than the other four petals thus making it slightly larger in shape. Pinch the edge of each petal to form a small stem.

A simple arrangement of yellow and orange pansies together with a Christmas rose, which is mounted on a painted circular box.

3. Place a small amount of glue on the stem of each petal. Attach the first two petals to the flower centre, one slightly behind the other.
4. Attach two more petals, one on either side and slightly behind the first two petals.
5. Attach the remaining slightly larger petal in the space which is left. (Diagram 31.)

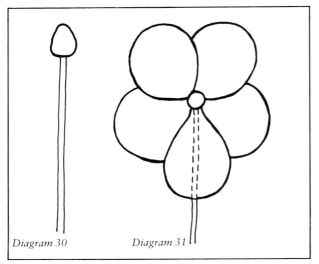

Diagram 30   *Diagram 31*

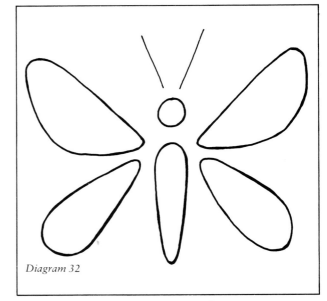

Diagram 32

Christmas rose

Flower centre

1. Make a rose centre as for the Dog rose on page 54. When dry, remove surplus net material.
2. Take a piece of yellow dough and roll it into a worm shape. Press flat and fringe very finely along one of the long edges.
3. Glue the uncut edge. Attach to the base of the flower centre. Pinch into place.
4. Using white dough, make six petals as for the Dog rose on page 54.
5. Attach three petals evenly spaced round the flower centre. Glue the remaining three petals in the spaces slightly behind the first three petals.

Calyx and leaves are made as for the rose.

Butterfly

Body section

1. Take a small piece of dough and roll it into a long thin capsule shape.
2. Take a very small piece of dough and roll it into a ball to form the head. Glue the head in position on the body.
3. To make antennae, cut two pieces of reel wire each 2cm long.
4. Place glue on the end of the wires and push the wires well into the head section, pointing them upwards.
5. When dry, paint the body black.

Wings

1. Flatten the dough and cut it into wing shapes as in Diagram 32.
2. Attach both sets of wings by glueing them in place slightly underneath the body. The lower wings are glued slightly underneath the larger, front pair of wings.
3. Leave to dry, then paint colours and patterns as desired. When dry, glaze.
4. Wings can be assembled in an upright position on the sides of the body as a variation. Support the wings on a bed of crumpled tissue paper until the glue is dry.

Butterflies look attractive attached to hairgrips, or on branches and twigs or in a flower arrangement.

Catkin spray

1. Select a delicate, willowy branch from a hazel or similar tree.
2. Take a piece of pale green dough the size of a walnut. Put the dough through a cheesemill or fine grinder or grater.
3. Gather up the small particles of dough lightly and gently together between the fingers. Without pressing too hard, form the dough into variously sized oblong shapes to resemble catkins. Be careful not to press the dough together too tightly, or it will lose its textured look.
4. While the catkins are still soft, glue them into little sprays of two and three, and glue them on the twigs.

Do not remove any buds which may be on the twigs as these enhance the natural appearance.

Press the arrangement into Plasticine, which can then be pressed into position on a piece of polished or natural wood to give a realistic appearance and a substantial base. Cover the Plasticine with moss or dried material.

To make the catkin spray less brittle and to preserve it, apply one or two coats of 50/50 solution of white glue and water.

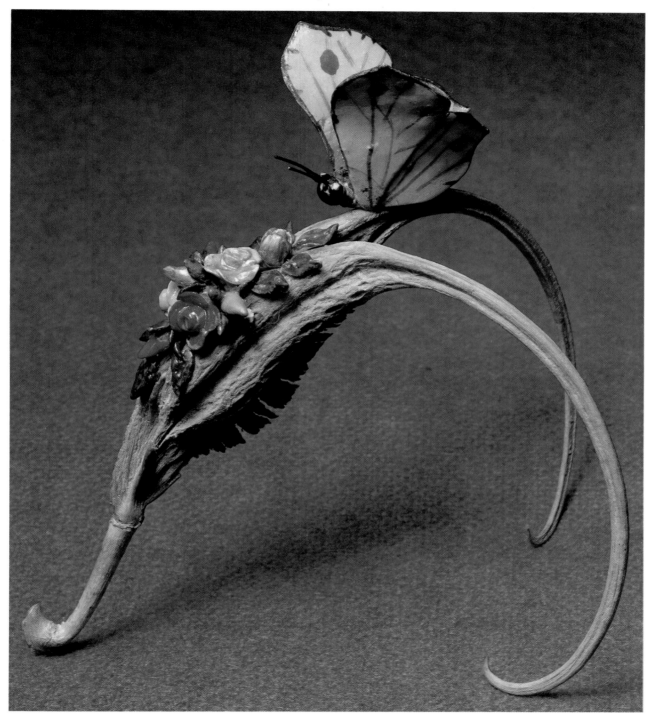

Perched on a dried plant is a brightly coloured winged insect. Children especially love to experiment with making insects such as ladybirds, bees or butterflies. They look particularly attractive when arranged on twigs amongst the blossom; or, indeed, when fastened to hair grips as a decoration.

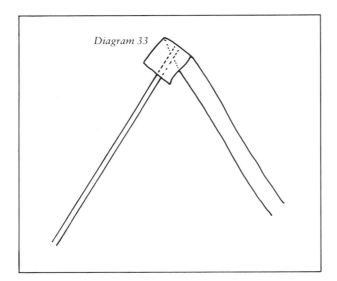

A small group of modelled flowers can be placed in a frame, recessed to hold protective glass. Dough can be pressed on to real leaves to give them realistic markings.

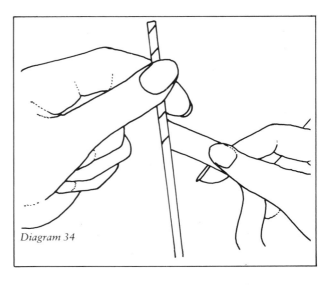

Covering flower wires (Diagrams 33 and 34)

Take a flower wire and cover the tip with floral tape. Spin the wire between finger and thumb, spiralling the tape down and along the wire to cover it tightly.

A posy of Marsh marigolds in a small bowl, and a tin decorated with Marsh marigolds and roses. Painting and then decorating used tins and boxes with bread dough flowers is an excellent way of making good use of them, and they make acceptable gifts or offerings for bazaars and sales of work.

Standing rose ornament

Make an attractive rose spray ornament. It forms an unusual and inexpensive gift, and a flower container is not required.

1. Make a rose and three buds in the usual way.
2. Make two small leaf sprays and wire them to the main rose stem just below the flower.
3. Make six individual leaves and wire them into position, evenly spaced between the rosebuds and just below the larger centre rose.
4. When the stems are gathered together, trim them all to the same length.
5. Bind all the stems together, leaving at least 2½cm unbound at the base which can be bent into position to form a firm standing base for the ornament.
6. Paint when dry, and allow paint to dry well before coating with varnish.

Holly (Diagram 35)

1. Take a piece of green dough and flatten it into an oblong shape. Cut into a leaf shape.
2. Remove six half moon sections from each side of this leaf shape.
3. Pinch the points of the serrated edges between the fingers to bring the leaves into a more realistic shape.
4. With a modelling tool, make a vein along the centre of the leaf.
5. Take a piece of reel wire and glue this to the centre back of the leaf and press reel wire well down into the leaf. Leave to dry, and paint dark green.
6. Make two more slightly smaller leaves the same way. Assemble into a leaf spray as described on page 53.
7. Make a few berries the size of small peas. Paint bright red. Glue into a central position well down along the leaf spray.
8. When dry, glaze as usual.

A silver spray of bread dough flowers and leaves in a glass makes a striking table arrangement for a festive occasion.

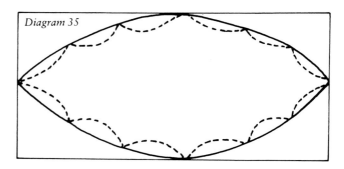

Diagram 35

PAPER FLOWERS

PAPER FLOWERS

Paper flowers are cheap, quick to make and can be made in colours to match any decor. In a few minutes, they can be made to go with table linen and china for a special dinner party. The worst they can do is fade! Coloured papers are manufactured in almost every colour imaginable. Select those which stimulate your imagination to invent beautiful or exotic or delicate plants. Discover the fun of creating your own plants and flowers.

The flower cone (pictured on page 71)

This is made by rolling a piece of 2½cm wire mesh netting into a cone. Protect your hands with garden gloves. Paint the mesh with adhesive, taking a small section at a time. Push a flower through each hole of the mesh, making sure that some of the petals stick to the wire. Completely cover the cone with flowers of different colours and varieties. This is a useful decoration for using up scraps of left-over paper. The cone can stand on its own or be hung with a ribbon attached to the top loop of the wire mesh. Patterns for crepe paper roses and anemones are shown on page 73 and diagrams for other flowers in Fig. 2.

   Make centres of fringed paper or make a ball centre. To do this, roll a piece of tissue paper into a ball and place it in a square of crepe paper. Twist the crepe round the ball of tissue and wire it tightly. Use it as it is, surrounded by a fringe of another colour, or dip the ball in glue and cover it with white sugar or Christmas glitter (see Fig. 1.).

Materials for making paper flowers

Scissors, wire cutters, heavy gauge wire (for stems), lightweight fuse wire (for binding), PVA adhesive or transparent glue, wire netting, egg boxes, sugar, dowelling, plaster and tin (for tree), cardboard, cartridge paper, tissue paper, crepe paper, gift-wrap ribbon, silver foil, pipe cleaners, paper doilies, bleach, paint brush, twigs, polythene bags.

Basic methods

All flowers and leaves are made in one of three basic ways. Flowers can be composed of individual petals wired together on a stem; they can be a long strip of crepe paper, scalloped and curled or just cut and then gathered on a stem; or they can be glued individually on wires and assembled around a stem.

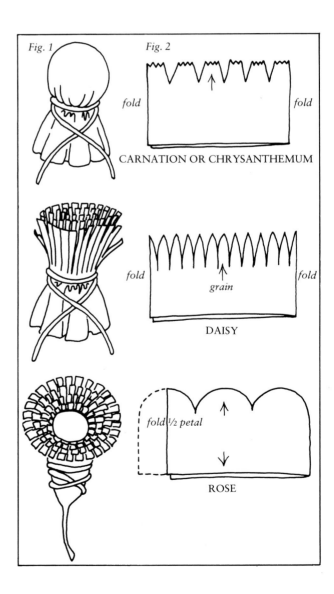

Fig. 1   Fig. 2

CARNATION OR CHRYSANTHEMUM

DAISY

ROSE

Method 1

Cut across a folded roll of crepe paper at least 6cm or 7cm wide. The width will determine the size of the finished flower. You can make petals larger, but 6–7cm is a good starting point for a rose, daisy or carnation of average size.

Cut the paper and bind it to the stem with fuse wire. The stem should be either heavy gauge wire or thick basket cane. For roses, cut a continuous strip of paper and scallop one edge of the 7cm strip, then curl the tops of the individual scallops by stroking with the thumb over a ruler or pair of scissors. Then gently stretch the base of each petal with both thumbs to provide an outward curve, and gather the petals around a stem.

A cone of brightly-coloured crepe and tissue paper flowers makes a pretty hanging decoration. The flowers are pushed through holes in the wire mesh, and the cone hangs from a ribbon.

You will need 10 to 12 petals to a rose and you can usually get 4 to 5 roses from one strip of an average roll of crepe paper (see Fig. 2).

Method 2

Cut individual petals (see page 73 for patterns). If the flower, for example a daisy, has a centre, the petals should be folded around the centre and when enough petals have been used, wired to the stem.

Method 3

Wire the paper. This is particuarly recommended for delicate papers like tissue which cannot hold their shape unsupported. Make a shape of the petal or leaf in a fairly heavy wire and leave a length over for the stem. (See page 74 for leaf and petal figs.) Cover the wire with glue and, when tacky, press on to a piece of crepe or tissue paper. Allow it to dry thoroughly then trim off the excess. The wire petal or leaf can be curved or twisted any way you choose.

To cover wire stems, cut a 1¼cm strip of crepe paper across the grain, put a little glue on the end and stick to the back of the flower head. Twist round the stem, stretching the paper gently until the wire is completely bandaged. If it is covering a leaf stem, start from the lower edge of the leaf. Glue the end

A simple arrangement of tissue paper flowers adds colour to a dark corner. Easily made of several large petals with long stamens, these flowers are wired to long stems.

and remember that you must plan the length of your stem before covering, because if you cut the stem you may undo the bandaging.

Tips to remember

Marked or crushed paper will not give you an exciting-looking flower, so try not to overwork your paper.

Strong sunlight will bleach coloured paper very quickly. PVA adhesive can be diluted with water or

used full strength. Although it is white and opaque, it dries clear and helps to strengthen the paper. Transparent glue is excellent for sticking, but not for sticking down layers of paper.

How to make the flowers

Daisy

Cut a length of heavy wire for the stem, then make a ball centre (Fig. 1). Zigzag and cut the edge of a 6cm strip of crepe paper and gather round the ball centre. Fasten with fuse wire and cover the stem with a strip of crepe. The leaves can be long narrow strips of crepe paper, narrowed to a point at one end, stuck in the stem while binding.

Anemone

Make a black ball centre of crepe and attach it to a wire. Surround the centre with black crepe fringe for stamens. Cut the petals (see Fig. 3, right) in pink, red or mauve. The number of anemone petals varies, here six are used. Curl and stretch the petals as for the rose and wire to a stem. Attach a calyx in green crepe and bind leaves to the stem while covering.

Rose 1

To make a strip rose, cut across a 6cm–7cm strip of crepe and scallop the edge (see Fig. 2 for pattern). Cut the petals and stretch them. Use fuse wire to attach to stem. Stick the calyx to the back of the rose and cover the stem with green crepe.

Rose 2

For separate petals, cut about 12–15 petals (see pattern right) and curl and stretch them as for the strip rose. To assemble the rose, roll one petal round itself to form a cone and arrange the other petals round this, slightly overlapping. Be sure to keep the tops of the petals level, otherwise the centre of the rose may protrude above them. Wire the petals to the stem and stick the calyx to the rose. Finish as for strip rose.

Carnation

Cut a 6cm–7cm strip across a roll of crepe with pinking shears (see Fig. 2) and cut back 2½cm at 1cm intervals along the strip. Stretch the strip slightly, curl the edges and gather round the stem. Use heavier wire to hold the flower together and make the wire long enough to form a stem. Stick the calyx to the back of the flower and add leaves while you are covering the stem.

You will know how long to cut the paper when you assemble this type of flower; the quality of paper varies so much that it is impossible to give exact measurements.

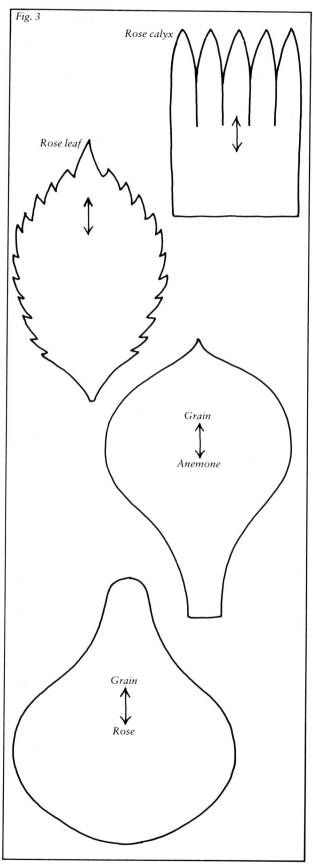

Fig. 3

Rose calyx

Rose leaf

Grain

Anemone

Grain

Rose

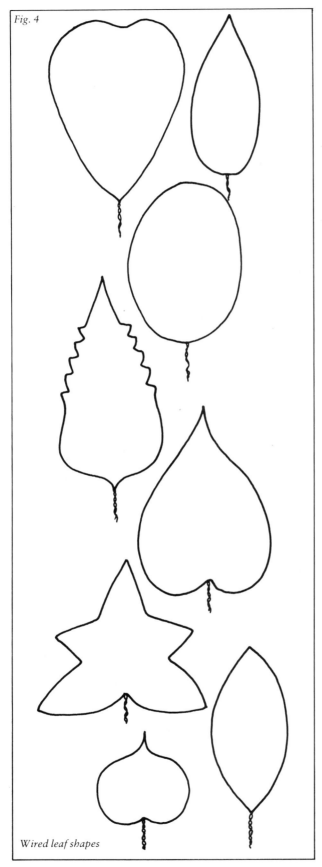

Fig. 4

Wired leaf shapes

Fig. 5

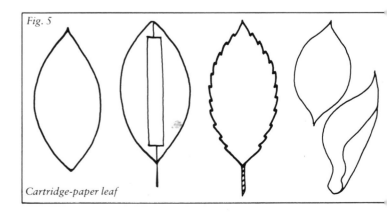

Cartridge-paper leaf

Leaves

Leaves can be made in many ways. The simplest way of all is to cut leaf shapes from crepe paper. If you are using duplex crepe, glue a wire down the middle of two leaf shapes. When dry, the leaf will bend.

A wire shape can also be made and covered in glue. While it is still tacky, place it on a larger piece of crepe paper and when it is completely dry, trim away the excess paper. (Fig. 4.)

The same principle can be applied when using tissue paper and this can be more exciting. When it is completely dry, paint the leaf with white PVA adhesive and stick over-layers of spots and stripes of different colours on to the leaf. Try laying on some lengths of thread. The adhesive will be milky in appearance when it is first applied, apparently removing the colour of the paper, but this is only temporary. Con-

This brilliant basketful of flowers includes carnations, anemones, roses and daisies. An ideal arrangement for hall or sitting-room.

A wreath made out of tissue-paper roses, arranged in the proper shape with a polystyrene base.

tinue overlaying and leave the leaf to dry before trimming off the excess paper. By then the paper will have become transparent again and quite firm.

To make cartridge paper leaves, cut out a leaf of the required shape and size, then lay a heavy stem wire down the whole of the middle length and cover with transparent tape. Trim and cut. (Fig. 5.)

Wired flowers

These involve exactly the same principle as for leaves, except that you may need more than one wired shape.

Look at the diagrams and invent your own flower. Decide how many petals it should have, how many shapes and what colours. When it is completely dry,

assemble it into a flower shape and wire to the stem. Cover the stem with crepe strip.

For both the wreath (above) and the ball of roses (page 77) use a strip of tissue paper which has first been scrunched up in your hand. Cut a strip measuring 30cm long and 5cm wide and on one side of the strip make 3cm deep cuts at 6cm intervals.

Lay a stocking knitting needle on the left-hand edge of the strip and roll half the 6cm section around the the next cut, in the opposite direction, and repeat the rolling-up process. Then scrunch up all the remaining

76

needle very tightly, as shown in Figure 6. Following the arrows, push both ends of the rolled-up paper towards each other (to give a crumpled effect) and then carefully draw out the needle. Lay the needle on

This delightful ball of tightly curled roses made of crepe paper makes an unusual hanging decoration. The leaves are made of tissue paper.

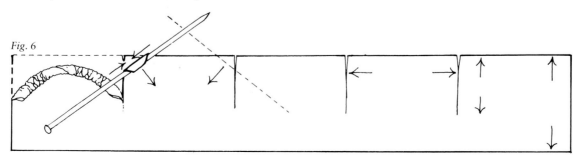

Fig. 6

petals and roll the first petal up to make the heart of the rose. Arrange the rest of the rose petals by gathering the edge of the strip around the centre and tying some fine wire around the end of the strip to secure it.

For instructions as to how to make the leaves, refer to the middle diagram in Figure 2, page 70. Use green strips measuring about 6cm long and 4cm wide. These are cut into leaf shapes on one edge and crumpled together on the other edge, which is then tied round with wire.

To make a wreath, use a wreath shape made of polystyrene, into which you push the ends of the wires, arranging leaves around each rose before sticking in the next wire. For the ball, the roses with their leaves

Paper can be used to make plants as well as flowers. This striking specimen is made by glueing tissue paper over wires and the stripes are achieved by bleaching.

are first wired to U-shaped pipe-cleaners, and the pipe-cleaners are then stuck into polystyrene.

Plants

This unusual looking plant with circular leaves is made with wired tissue.

To obtain good wire circles, bend the wire around

bottles and containers, twist the wires and slip them off the containers. Use small containers for small leaves and increase the size as desired for larger leaves.

Before glueing or adding overlays, the leaves are bleached in circles. Use ordinary domestic bleach, and a very old brush, washing it at once after use. Allow the bleach to dry completely, then proceed as follows.

(*Note*. It is not advisable to use bleach when working with young children. Bleach has to be used full strength for effect and it can burn if it touches the skin. It can also cause damage if it splashes the eyes.)

The plant with the pointed leaves (see above) is also made of tissue paper on wire with glued overlays. Cut as many wire leaves as you need, starting with very small ones for the top of the plant and increasing in

Another unusual plant decoration, with spotted and multi-coloured leaves. These are made by glueing layers of tissue paper on top of each other on wire frames.

size towards the bottom. Only when each leaf is finished, trimmed and dried do you assemble the plant.

Start at the top of the plant and work down, bandaging the stem with crepe paper as you go down. When the plant is complete, stand it in a tin or plastic carton filled with plaster or something heavy to make it stable.

Cartridge paper flowers

Cartridge paper has no stretching qualities so the flowers and leaves made from it have to be simple and stylised.

For a lily shape, cut a quarter section from a fairly large circle (tea-plate size), scallop the edge, roll round into a cone shape and stick one side to the other. Leave a small hole for the stem to pass through. The stamen can be a straight fringe gathered into a bunch and attached to the stem. The daisy is a long strip with zig-zags cut on one edge and cuts made into each petal. This, too, surrounds the fringe centre.

Flat wall plaques can be made by arranging flowers and leaves in an attractive pattern on a circle of strong

Cartridge paper flowers can provide a contrast to crepe and tissue paper flowers and in their way they are just as attractive. This is an arrangement of daffodils in a paper vase.

cardboard. Start by sticking from the outside of the plaque and working towards the centre. Such plaques can look very pretty if sprayed gold or silver, and they make unusual Christmas decorations. A hanging loop can be attached to the back.

The daffodils above are cut in two sections, one for the petals, which are scored down the middle to give variety to their surfaces, and the trumpets, which are

Fig. 7a

Fig. 7b

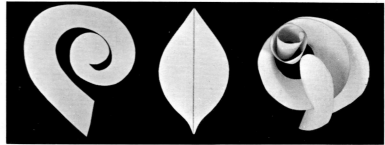

Fig. 7c

cones (see Fig. 7a above). The leaves are long and pointed.

A fluted paper vase is an ideal setting for an arrangement of this kind.

The rose

Roll the paper into a cone from the outside. As you 'lift' the outside of the paper over the centre of the rose, it will hold it together. (Fig. 7c.)

This sort of flower is not really suitable for vases, and looks better flat on a base. The leaves are simple shapes folded in half and then opened. The outsides of the leaves can be curled. (Fig. 7b.)

Striped flowers

Make a ball centre for each flower and dip them with glue and cover them with tiny, finely cut squares of dif-

ferent coloured crepe paper. Fringe the centre with tissue paper. Cut large petals in dark coloured crepe and paint each one with stripes in domestic bleach. When dry, and the stripes have bleached white, curl, stretch and wire them to the back of the ball centre. Cover the stems with crepe strips.

Blossom

Cut some simple pink flowers from tissue paper (fold the sheet of tissue into small squares so that you can cut out a lot at a time). Stick the flowers in groups on to a natural twig. Choose a dainty twig to match the delicacy of the tissue paper. Cut tiny circles of orange cardboard from an old food packet and stick them to the centre of the flowers.

The clear, bold colours of tissue and crepe papers
make beautiful stylised flower arrangements. You
can use several different colours for the petals or cut
them all in one shade.

FEATHER FLOWERS

FEATHER FLOWERS

Nearly everyone admires the varied and subtle qualities of a bird's plumage, but few people realise how the feathers can be used for decorative purposes. Close inspection reveals an astonishing range of shapes, sizes and patterns which can be used to produce extraordinarily effective and impressive designs.

Types of feather

Feathers fall into two major categories; flight feathers, which are stiff enough to support the birds in flight, and contour feathers, which cover the body like clothing. The latter tend to be fluffy for warmth and curved to fit the contours of the body closely. There are several kinds of feather within these two categories. Only tail and crest feathers are straight. Tail feathers act as a form of balancing rudder for the bird in flight (Fig. 1). Wing feathers curve slightly sideways according to which side of the bird they come from. These feathers undulate and interlock (Fig. 2). Both these types of strong feathers are suitable for leaf shapes and other designs. The body feathers curve to a greater or lesser degree according to the part of the bird from which they come; they will also curve sideways. If you compare a back feather with a breast feather, the difference is apparent immediately (Fig. 3). Feathers with these curves can be used as petals.

When birds have moulted you can see the extraordinary markings of the patterned feathers. Pheasants (the peacock, golden pheasant, ring-neck etc.) have the most striking patterns on their feathers. The ring-neck pheasant has goldside, red-heart and church-window feathers; there are corresponding feathers on the other two birds. There are other exotic pheasants: Impeyan, Reeves, Silver and Lady Amherst. If you are lucky enough to obtain any of the rare feathers from these birds, you can use them as a prominent feature of a design.

Do not ignore domestic birds. Their plumage can be as varied if not so striking as that of the rarer birds. Goose feathers are best for craft work, but chicken and turkey feathers are equally adaptable. They are strong and plain and therefore suitable for dyeing. Not all domestic feathers are plain, however, chickens as we know them are descended from jungle fowl, whose tiny striped feathers are most attractive, as are the

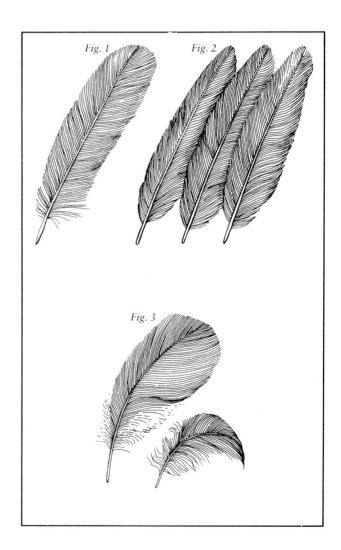

spotted feathers of the guinea fowl. Partridges, of which there are several kinds, have a few striped but delicately shaded feathers on their sides. The duck family have very soft feathers with an abundance of down, their protective layer against cold water. Mallard have softly mottled feathers, and each teal breast feather has one tiny spot.

A visit to the zoo will no doubt produce a specially treasured feather for a design. Look out for crest

feathers and the red spears from the side of a golden pheasant tail. This bird also has vivid orange and black collar feathers.

It is vitally important to remember that, however concentrated your feather collecting becomes, it must in no way harm the birds. Feathercraft uses *discarded* feathers.

Handling feathers

Feathers are composed of rows of tiny feathers, connected to a central vein. Each tiny feather, known as a bract, has a row of hooks on each side which interlock with their neighbours (Fig. 4, next page). When the top part of the feather fuses, the hooks engage and make the feather smooth. Where the hooks remain separate the feather is fluffy. Ostrich wings are the largest example of this type (Fig. 5).

The hollow part of the feather can be used to attach a feather to a wire stem. Cut the tip off and insert the wire into the cavity (Fig. 6).

A small number of feathers from a peacock's magnificent plumage have been assembled to make this design on a piece of wood. Back feathers are used for the flowers in a curved line. The blue flowers are made with feathers from further down the bird's back. The tumbling stamens come from the side of the tail feathers, three of which are placed at the bottom between the leaves, which are cut from wing feathers. The peacock's entire plumage seems blue and green, but he has brown wings and some speckled feathers and no design would be complete without this pleasing contrast.

You can make a quill pen by trimming off the tip of a feather. Take a slanting piece from the back before making a small slit in the nib part to enable the ink to flow freely (Fig. 7).

When you cut feathers, always use a very sharp instrument. Feathers are surprisingly tough and the spring in the contour part can lead to inaccuracy, so

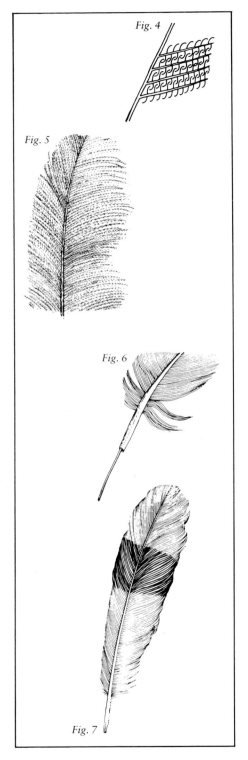

Fig. 4

Fig. 5

Fig. 6

Fig. 7

It is surprising how much variety there is in the ring-necked pheasant's plumage. Flowers assembled from as many different feathers as possible are unusually attractive. This dome of flowers on a candlestick has been designed to stand at the centre of the dining table. Flowers on their own tend to allow too much wire stem to show, so a few feather leaves have been added to combat this.

cut firmly. You can trim feathers into many shapes, but cut the whole side at one go with large, sharp scissors.

A thin point is elegant on a leaf but tends to be too severe for petals which need to be more rounded (Fig. 8). When choosing feathers, use only the best; poor ones make poor flowers.

When making a leaf, having shaped the top, strip away the lower part to leave a realistic shape standing on its own stem (Fig. 9). A bunch of these made from tiny feathers can be assembled for use as stamens.

All feathers have natural curves, but you can add more. Hold the feather on to the blade of a blunt knife or pair of scissors, squeeze the vein along its length

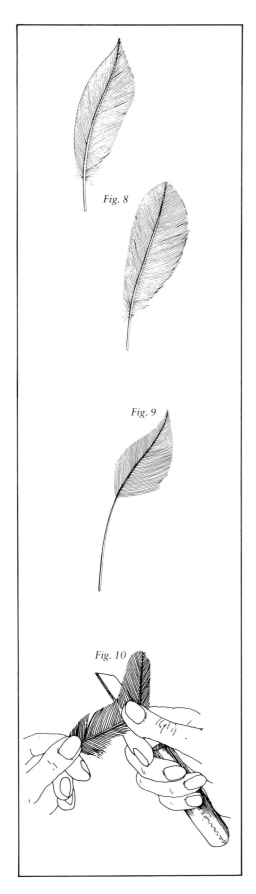

Fig. 8

Fig. 9

Fig. 10

Allia are a type of onion with erect stems supporting a ball of tiny flowers. In June, these pink, white or purple flowers enhance the herbaceous border. These feathered versions are really many little flowers, assembled into a ball and attached to a stem. At the centre of each is a small piece of marabou, which will quiver in the slightest draught.

until you get the required curve (Fig. 10). Do not pull the feather or you may destroy the contour. Repeat the action until you are satisfied. If the bracts separate, coax them together by pulling so that the little hooks re-engage. This is a simple movement originally intended to be made by a beak.

Flower centres

The centre, the focal point around which the petals are wrapped to encase the seed, is a very important part of a flower. However small it is, it should be prominent and easily recognisable in a design. But there are exceptions to every rule and such flowers as roses and carnations have too many petals for the centre to be visible amongst the profusion of layers. Choose a material that blends or contrasts with the petals, according to the type of flower you are imitating.

Small whole dried flowers are suitable and a cluster standing in the centre of the petals can look charming (Fig. 11). Bind a bunch very tightly to the top of a stem wire with binding wire before adding the petals. Alternatively, the centre can act as a receptacle for feather petals; you can use one of the many types of fir cone for this purpose.

Choose one similar in size to the petals you want to use. It will probably have lost its stem, so make a hook at the top of a stem wire and insert it between the lower scales of the fir cone (Fig. 12).

You can also use feathers for the centres (as in the pictures right). If you make a bunch of peacock or ostrich bracts, curl them over scissors so that the resulting spirals tumble outwards over the petals (Fig. 13). Some flat and shiny feathers contrast very well with a very fluffy centre. For this type of centre you can use marabou feathers which have such a soft texture that one would fill the centre of most lilies (Fig. 14).

If, after a day at the zoo or a jumble sale, you obtain one or two very special feathers, use them for the centre and choose some appropriate petals to go with them (Fig. 15).

As a general guide, the centre (stamens or stems) should be in proportion to the area covered by the petals. Also, consider the outline of your flower in profile, for it will be looked at from many angles.

Beads. Since they are small shiny objects, beads form a perfect contrast to soft feathers. Massed together or used separately, they can be put on their own wire stems so that they stand above, rather than get lost among, the fluff at the bottom of the feathers. Pearls, for example, combined with white feathers, are perfect centres for wedding flowers. At Christmas, when a metallic element is needed for decorations, gold or silver beads look festive and enable you to avoid ruining the texture of the feathers by painting them or sticking things into them (Fig. 16).

Examples of different flower centres. Top: *curled bracts tumbling out over the petals.* Middle: *fluffy soft textured feathers contrasting well with flat and shiny feathers, and,* bottom, *tightly curled feathers surrounded by smooth flat ones.*

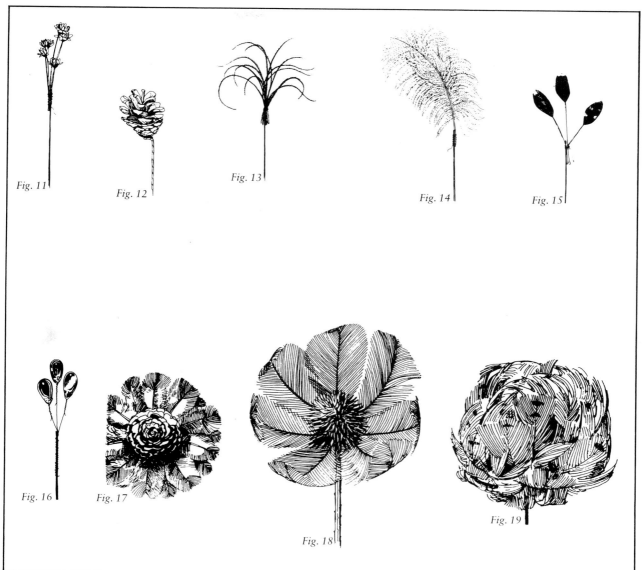

Fig. 11

Fig. 12

Fig. 13

Fig. 14

Fig. 15

Fig. 16

Fig. 17

Fig. 18

Fig. 19

Flowers and glue

If you use a fir-cone centre, remember that the choice of cone determines the type of feathers you put with it. For example, if you have small larch cones, choose pigeon-body feathers or something similar (Fig. 17). Use a clear plastic impact glue if possible. Apply it carefully, well in between the scales, and push the bottom tip of the feathers right into it. Assemble your petals first and, if necessary, cut the ends off to unify the lengths before applying the glue.

Teazles are another type of seed-head with many scales to hold feathers. Because of their shape and size, these require large, flat goose shoulder or similar feathers. Trim the edges to tidy the outline and attach them to the teazle with glue. If the curve in the petals is irregular when the flower is assembled, curl the straighter ones carefully when in position (Fig. 18).

One of the easiest methods of making flowers is to use florist's foam (such as Styrofoam or Oasis in the UK) as a centre core into which to push the feathers. These materials are available in ready-shaped spheres, but if you have a melon ball cutter you can easily cut your own shapes from large pieces. Cover your stem wire before glueing it to the ball, because wire glued to foam will work loose after a short time. Start in the centre at the top, dip the tops of the feathers into a little glue and push them into the ball until it is sufficiently covered. Tiny feathers, such as the curly duck or teal breast feathers, can be used in this way to make a small red rose (Fig. 19).

Alternatively, fill the centre with small dried flowers,

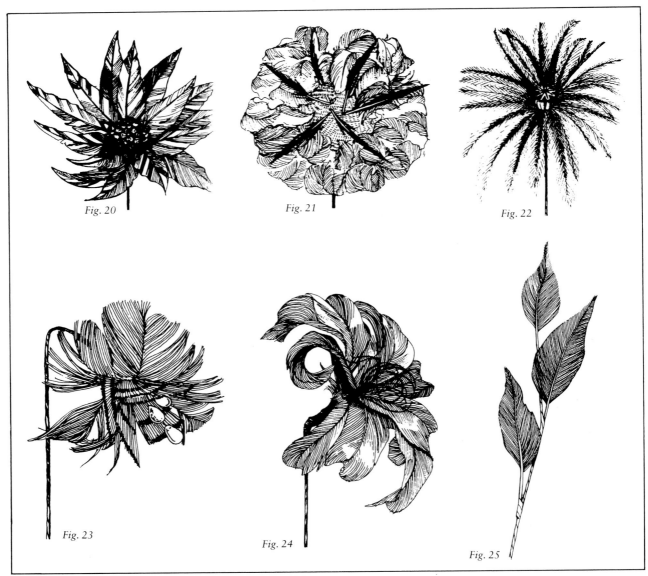

Fig. 20

Fig. 21

Fig. 22

Fig. 23

Fig. 24

Fig. 25

then bind the petals to the stem below the centre. These larger flowers have a striking appearance, suitable for a large hall or as stage decorations (Fig. 20).

Larger foam spheres for bridesmaids are more readily available. They are intended to bear a covering of tiny flowers, dried or otherwise. The entire shape is probably too large for most flowers, so cut it in half. During assembly, especially if you use a lot of feathers, the stem often works loose, so work with the foam flat on the table and add the stem afterwards. The flower resulting from this size of centre is large and working with it flat on the table is a help in keeping the flowers level. The combinations are limitless, so experiment with the various feathers at your disposal.

When you are ready to add the stem, cover three wires together, leaving 2½cm fanned out at the top. Glue the three tips to the back of the flower to prevent the heavy head from twisting round on the stem. You

can cover the foam that is still visible by glueing some feathers flat onto it (Fig. 21).

Flowers and binding wire

If you find working with glue messy, assemble your flowers with wire. Use a very fine wire for the binding and a much heavier straight one for the stem. If the gauges are too close to each other, the binding wire may distort the stem wire, which should stay rigid. To avoid a disappointing collapse when the flower is complete, bind each feather firmly in position and do not let it rotate with the binding motion. Keep the same piece of binding wire throughout the flower assembly and try to avoid superfluous binding; it creates a bulky joint below the petals.

When you have chosen a centre, add the required number of petals. Thin feathers are a suitable shape for a daisy, but make the petals horizontal (Fig. 22).

Many hand-made flowers are round, so try bending yours to point downwards. The most satisfactory element of a flower in this position is a bunch of pendant stamens.

In a fuchsia, for example, the sepals are incorporated into the design, and that allows a combination of two layers of petals with the stamens. The final layer should curl back sufficiently to allow the rest of the flower to be seen clearly (Fig. 23).

Use flat sattins to make lilies, and curl them until you have enough multiples of six to assemble (Fig. 24). The number of petals should be the same as, or a multiple of, the number of stamens. In the lily family, which should have six petals, the number of stamens is six and the petals six or twelve. If you need five petals, assemble them around a single centre.

A close-up of some spectacular chrysanthemum type flowers, made out of red and cream feathers, making a splash of colour that even nature would find it hard to imitate.

Leaves

Single feathers from exotic birds can be used in their entirety or parts can be stripped from the central vein. Some of the ostrich family, and peacocks, have long feathers with separate bracts to which you can add a little variety by curling them all the way up. Pheasant tail feathers can look a little severe, but if you strip one side and curl the whole length, they add big swirling lines to a cluster of flowers. Small feathers can be assembled on wire stems as sprays of leaves. Simply join each leaf in during the stem binding. (Fig. 25).

Dyeing feathers

Nature produces an astonishing array of patterns and colours, but at times you will want to change them. Feathers dye very easily; you can use a hot water fabric dye and follow the instructions on the packet. It is important to boil the feathers because this breaks down their water resistance (which will vary according to whether they come from land or water birds). Once you are satisfied that they have absorbed all the dye, put the feathers on absorbent paper (for instance, newspaper) in front of a fan heater or hair dryer and blow them dry. That should restore the fluff but if you are not satisfied, you can hold the feather in steam for half a minute to allow the little hooks to stand up again. If you have a lot of feathers to steam,

Used carefully, feather fluff can look charming; the added contrast of some strong flat feathers often emphasizes its softness. The big flowers with goose nagoire shoulder feathers are filled with a profusion of marabou in the centre. Ostrich feathers and white turkey feathers, are contrasted with dark lilies made from curled goose satin wing feathers.

bring a preserving pan of water to the boil and place a wire cake tray on the top for the feathers to lie on. When steaming your feathers, do not get impatient and stroke them before they are fully dry.

SEED FLOWERS

SEED FLOWERS

Delightful two-dimensional and three-dimensional flowers can be made out of the different types of seeds that are available from the garden and the kitchen.

A fortunate aspect of seed mosaic is that the raw materials are so easy to come by. We plant some of the prettiest specimens in the garden; we cook them and we feed them to domestic animals. If you look at them closely, you will see that most of them are very attractive in themselves, both in colour and shape. When placed together in groups of one kind or in a combination of types, they offer a wide variety of pattern, shape and texture that is difficult to obtain by other methods. The inherent charm and variety of seeds make work with them an excellent craft for those who are doubtful of their ability to invent their own designs, for the simplest of stripes, chevrons or circles often make the most effective patterns and demand no great artistic talent.

Seed mosaic is surely also one of the most economical of crafts for most suitable seeds cost little and those you can find in the fields or garden cost nothing at all. Even the most expensive can be bought in small quantities.

Equipment needed for the craft is minimal, and the work is very clean, for, once you learn to control the amounts of glue used, there are no other hazards.

All the seeds used here are available almost anywhere. In some countries you may find more exotic varieties. If you cannot obtain the precise kinds seen here, then experiment and use your ingenuity to make similar patterns with those which you can find.

If you are concerned about the permanency of your products, artists say that many of their seed decorations have lasted for years. The seeds do not disintegrate, even though sometimes their colours may change slightly. Essentially, seed mosaic work is a 'fun' craft, and the most important thing is to enjoy doing it and be pleased with the results.

Seeds to use

First of all, you have to find the seeds. If you have a garden and it happens to be autumn, you can start in the garden. Alternatively go out for a walk in the country and see how many different sorts of seeds you can find there.

Collect and hang up to dry any seed heads with a good shape or interesting content. Poppy seed heads are nearly always an attractive shape and they come in many sizes.

The seeds inside Honesty are so pretty that it is worth going to the trouble of getting them out. Whenever you have the opportunity, collect fir cones, acorns and their cups, sycamore wings and ash wings, which come in a great variety of shapes and colours, and pieces of the spiky branches of the monkey puzzle tree. Sunflower seeds are an attractive shape and size.

Other sources of supply are corn or seed merchants and large pet shops or animal feed suppliers. Ask permission to look in the seed bins for suitable specimens. You should find wheat, groats, maple peas, white and striped sunflower seeds, niger, black and red rape, paddy rice, tares, milo, black eye beans and millet without any difficulty. From shops specialising in foreign foods, from health food shops selling natural and compost-grown foods, you can get Chinese lentils, European lentils, small orange lentils, brown, red, white and black beans, soya beans, moth beans, mung beans, large and small split peas in greens and yellows, pale green flageolet beans, and golden sweet corn. Your grocer will be able to supply you with the more homely domestic seeds.

If you eat melons or pumpkins, keep the seeds, wash them and lay them out on a flat surface to dry before putting them into a jar to store for your collection. Buy or collect new seeds wherever you find them and keep them in screw-topped jars labelled with their names.

Equipment

Most of what you need will be in your house already. Gather everything together and find a work surface where you can leave things between sessions.

Glue. PVA medium is the most effective. It dries clear, colourless and invisible and is very strong. When mixed with water in a solution of one part medium to two parts water, it becomes a protective varnish for the finished work. Squeeze the glue out a little at a time and replace the top of the jar or tube. It dries out quickly.

Craft knife. One with a replaceable blade is very useful for splitting and trimming seeds.

Tooth picks. Pointed at one end, flat at the other, these will help you put the glue where you want it and also to pick up the smallest seeds.

Strong card. Rectangles about 25mm × 51mm are useful for spreading larger areas of glue. You will also need cardboard for flower backings.

Tweezers. To pick up and position seeds which are too small to handle with the fingers.

Flower wires. For flower stems.

Green binding to bind the stems. (Buy it from florists.)

Pencil, ruler, scissors, elastic bands, white paper.

Clear Polyurethane varnish.

Brush for varnishing.

Containers for seeds, empty pill boxes, jars etc.

A vase of seed flowers can look very pretty. Mounted on a base made out of cardboard or a large button, the seeds are carefully arranged in layers of different colours and shapes, giving the impression of small sunflowers.

Varnishing

Varnishing serves several purposes. The varnish increases the richness of the colour of the seeds and it protects them from dust and to some extent, from damage. It keeps the small seeds securely in place. Once varnished, they are not only fixed from below but they are covered by a thin protective glaze. This

Seed flower medallions are ideal for decorating your Christmas tree. Use cardboard discs to make the base, and glue on the seeds and beans in patterns.

enables your flowers and pictures to be dusted from time to time without fear of the seeds falling off.

How to begin

Before trying to make any sort of picture or flower, take a piece of cardboard or perhaps a rectangular cork mat and play with the seeds on it for a while. Start with the middle-sized and bigger ones and arrange them in strips of different widths and simple groups until you get the knack of handling them. Then fix them with glue. For a more elaborate design, try folding and cutting a piece of paper. Cut boldly but simply into the folded paper, then open it out to see the total design. Make as many attempts as you need, then

interpret the shape into seeds. Work the pattern in loose seeds on a piece of felt, or set them lightly into a sheet of Plasticine. Then copy the design on to its permanent background.

Sticking

Use the end of the toothpick to apply glue on small area. Place the larger seeds one at a time with the

96

An usual idea for a wall decoration, for anyone who has a woodworker in the family. Seeds and beans are set in little recessed plaques, where their colours harmonise with those of the natural wood.

fingers or tweezers. For larger shapes, built up from very small seeds, make the shape in glue first, then sprinkle it with seeds, pushing them together. A tiny spot of glue on the end of a toothpick will enable you to pick up single small seeds. Give the end of the toothpick a lick, then dip it into small seeds and you will be able to pick up about a dozen at a time, placing them on to the ready-glued surface rapidly.

Making flowers

A vase of seed flowers can look very pretty and need not be too hard to make. Use a large button or a circle of strong cardboard as a base for the seed petals. Thread it first with strong flower wire, to act as a stem.

Bind the stem with green florist's binding, or with strips of brown or green crepe paper wound tightly round the wire. Start on the outside of the button or cardboard and stick on a layer of petals. Work towards the centre with circles of different coloured and shaped seeds. Flowers like this make lovely Christmas decorations, and also form attractive arrangements for a vase, when mixed with dried leaves or even fresh ones (see pictures on next page).

Flowers always make an attractive gift. Make a
bouquet using covered wire as a stem, and blossoming
twigs and branches. The flowers are formed by
dipping a ball of cotton wool, covered with glue, into
a jar of poppy seeds. Surround these with barley or
cucumber seeds.

PLASTIC & 'DIPIT' FLOWERS

PLASTIC & 'DIPIT' FLOWERS

Thanks to a new, fast-drying liquid acrylic plastic film, anyone can make the beautiful flowers described in this chapter. The film is not expensive to buy in craft shops and a few hours' practice will give enormous pleasure and decorative results.

This plastic film is available throughout the world, in various colours, and with translucent or opaque effects. It is sold under different names such as 'Liquid dip film,' or trade names like 'Fantasy film', 'Dip-it', 'Whimsy Dip', and 'Dippity Glas'. It comes in bottles and cans. When spread across a wire shape (circle, oval, or triangle) it dries to a wafer-thin film giving the effect of translucent or opaque gaily-coloured glass. Different shapes and colours can be used in various permutations and patterns to make attractive floral arrangements. Flower petals and leaves are easy to simulate and you can copy real flowers, or experiment and create your own floral fantasies.

Materials

Liquid plastic dipping solution
Copper, brass or aluminiun wire in different gauges
Wire cutters or old scissors
A piece of polystyrene foam, or a potato
Flower stamens or centres
Florist's wire for stems
Floral tape or raffia
Strengthener and thinners (optional)

Wire

The gauge of wire will decide the type of film you make. A thick wire will give a thick film and a thick border. For small petals and leaves, 28 SWG wire is adequate. Larger shapes need a heavier gauge (about 18) to withstand the strain. Copper and aluminium are easy to form into shapes but they can be distorted when they are used for large areas. If you want to cover a large area, use galvanised iron wire. Beginners should really start on smaller flowers, with thin wire.

Dipping (see diagrams on page 102)

Fig. 1. Make a loop and twist the wire several times at the base to form a stem several inches long. (You need

this stem to hold the shape of the petal.) Dip this wire shape into the coloured liquid. The simplest way to do this is to dip the shape into the film and draw it upwards, letting the film run off the tip. Hold it until it stops dripping, then stick the stem upright into a polystyrene tile or potato to dry (five to ten minutes). If a drip is left at the tip, snip it off with scissors when dry. This method produces a dark tip and a light base.

Fig. 2. The second method is to dip the wire shape into the liquid film and then tip the petal upwards so that the tip is higher than the base and the excess liquid runs towards the base of the stem. Wipe the excess off on the edge of the can. Push the wire into a polystyrene tile or potato to dry. This method gives a dark base and a light tip. If the petal or stem is very long, tip the can while dipping.

Fig. 3. This method is used for large shapes and gives an even film. Bend the stem 90 degrees to the plane of the shape and hold the wire horizontally above the liquid. Submerge the shape horizontally and remove it horizontally. The excess liquid forms a slight drip at the centre. For large shapes, pour the liquid film on to a dinner plate, to give a better working area.

Fig. 4. Make circular leaf and petal wire shapes around a 'former', such as a cardboard tube. This will produce even, uniform shapes. You can then turn these circles into pointed leaves and petals by pulling at them with a bradawl or a knitting needle.

Making shapes

You can repeat the same shapes by using patterns traced on paper. You may need a jig for complex shapes but an inexpensive one can be improvised by sticking nails into thick polystyrene foam, round which the wire can be formed.

Curved shapes produce attractive effects in the film. Unless you want special effects, it is usually better to curve the shapes before the film dries, for once it is dry it may crinkle and break. Shapes are curved uniformly by curling them around a cylinder.

100

A set-piece arrangement of larkspur, described on page 104-5.

General tips

Do not try to cover very large areas. The entire shape (including several twists of the stem) must be submerged in the liquid or the film will not form, and this is difficult when the shape is very large.

If the film breaks before it is completely removed from the liquid, simply re-dip until it forms a complete film, but do not touch the side of the can when removing the wire or the film certainly will break.

Exposure of the liquid film to air thickens the plastic, so close the can lid when the film is not in use.

Natural streaks may occur from time to time, but these will enhance the colourful effects of the petals and leaves. Sometimes bubbles will appear while dipping, and this is usually caused by dipping too quickly. The bubbles will go if the liquid is left to stand for a few minutes, but again, the bubbles will enhance the flowers, giving a Venetian glass effect.

You can toughen flower petals and leaves by dipping them in strengthener or by dipping petals and leaves a second time 24 hours after the first dip. This will give a double coating without spoiling the delicate glass look of the film. Before using strengthener, allow the shapes to dry for 45 minutes. The strengthener itself takes 1–2 hours to dry.

Special effects

Curve and twist petals and leaves to give a graceful, three-dimensional effect. Look at flowers, trees and shrubs for inspiration. Nature rarely creates a dull, flat shape. Twist wire before or (very carefully) after dipping. The former gives smooth, taut shapes, the latter causes wrinkles and waves in the film.

Make small flowers of clusters of leaves in one operation by winding the wire around a cylindrical shape 1–2cm in diameter (a pen or small bottle will serve).

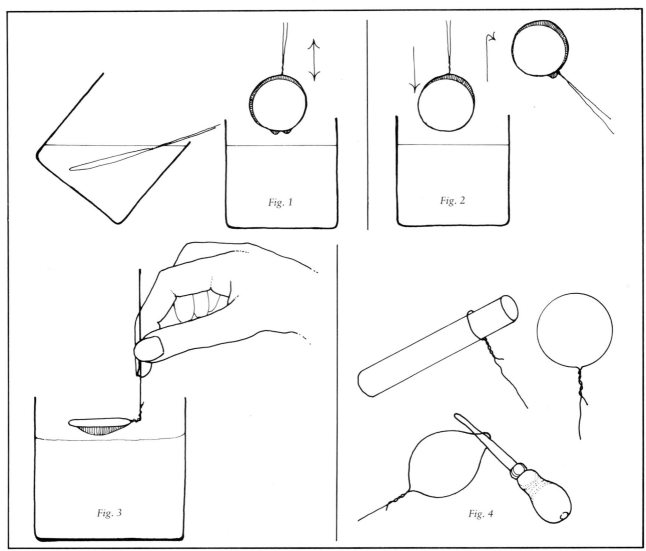

Fig. 1

Fig. 2

Fig. 3

Fig. 4

Twist the ends of the wire to form the stem; remove from the cylinder and open out, giving each section a final twist.

Wavy or ruffled edges can be made by winding the wire around a very thin pencil or nail. Remove and extend the coil, then form your chosen shape (see diagrams opposite).

Quick dipping puts streaks in to the film. They can resemble the veins in leaves. Try pouring a little liquid of one colour on to another colour. Stir a little, then dip. This will produce multi-coloured streaks useful for all kinds of fantasy creations. You can paint the dried film with most oil-based or acrylic paints, but try them out first, as not all paints are compatible with acrylic film. You can decorate the film with felt-tipped pens.

Unusual and spectacular results can be achieved with the use of gold and silver glitter. Sprinkle it on while the film is still tacky. You can also shake on glitter when the strengthener is drying. Glitter is especially suitable for Christmas decorations.

Bright copper or plastic-coated wire can be used instead of usual silver-coloured wire, to make coloured borders. Or try stringing the wire with bugle or rocaille beads before dipping them in the plastic.

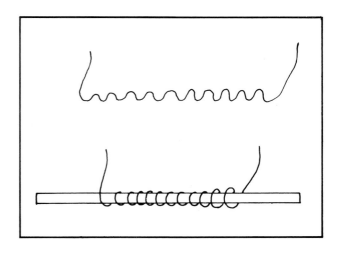

Flowers

Once you have mastered the simple skill of dipping and seen the different shapes it is possible to produce, you can start to make more ambitious flowers and floral arrangements. Flowers are always a popular choice and a carefully designed flower set-piece, ablaze with brilliant translucent blooms, will enhance every corner of the home.

If you become very adept, you will soon be able to produce life-like floral arrangements, but if realism is what you seek, then you should study the forms and colours of real flowers. Go into the garden and observe the shapes of the flowers and leaves there; look at gardening books and seed catalogues; read reference books. For realism, you need a sharply observant eye.

All flowers need centres or stamens. Some handi-craft shops sell ready-made stamens, but you can easily make your own. Beads on the end of a piece of wire (coiled or straight), chenille, cotton balls, ribbon

An arrangement of tea roses and forget-me-nots and a wreath. See page 107.

bows, feathers or knotted wire dipped in liquid film all make suitable centres. Other sections of this book will also give you good ideas for flower stamens.

Assembling flowers

Use a 16–18 SWG wire for your stem. Then assemble the centre and the petals and bind the wire ends with florist's tape. Tie them around the stem. Bind the rest of the stem, adding leaves where you want them. Make sure everything is tightly bound and secure it firmly with a knot or glue at the base of the stem.

Set pieces

Before starting on any 'set piece', always decide what colours, how many pieces and the shapes you need.

Make a rough sketch if you can, as this can be helpful.

Vary your flower containers if possible. On page 109 you see a beautiful arrangement in ice-cold colours, which has been mounted on glass and above is another lovely group of flowers, simply arranged round a candle.

Plain wood looks well as a base for flowers of most kinds. Use strong glue to hold the flowers in position. Dried natural flowers can look very pretty mixed with dipped flowers, as can grasses and poppy seed heads.

Small baskets also are an excellent setting for floral pieces and plants can be made to twine round the handles in a rustic way. A wall decoration, such as a wooden trellis intertwined with fantasy flowers, is always popular.

Try to vary all the shapes of the different flowers in an arrangement and avoid having a large number of the same flowers, or flowers of the same colour, in

Some basic shapes for leaves and flowers. Looking at natural forms will give you ideas for inventions of your own. Even if the one illustrated on page 107 in colour seems elaborate, you will find such inventions easy once you are skilled in forming and combining all kinds of shapes.

one vase, as this makes for monotony.

For a natural look, make sure you bend stems and leaves, rather than leave them stiff and upright, for this is not nature's way.

Colourful larkspur arrangement
(picture page 101)

The top row of three sketches on page 106 shows how to make up the larkspurs starting with the individual petals. Once all the flowers are made, they are attached

Top left: *Basket of daisies. Thread a bead on to some wire and attach 10–13 individual daisy petals. Wind florist's tape around the wire stem, and press some Plasticine into the glass basket. Stick the individual flower stems into the Plasticine and decorate the edge of the basket with a bow.*

along a thick piece of wire. Cover the wire with green florist's tape.

The yellow flowers have six petals, which are rolled inwards before being tied together to make up the flower head. The white flowers have a pale green centre and either three or six petals each. Cover a plate with aluminium foil and, on top of this, place some Plasticine. Arrange the single twigs and flowers either as in the illustration or according to your own design.

Top right: *Decoration for a present – arrange the flower petals around the beads and twist the wire round to secure. Make 10–15 loops with a length of lace, and twist some wire around them to make a flat bouquet. Decorate the long stem with a big bow.*

Bottom right: *Basket of flowers. This is a simple dipit project. For the centre of these multi-coloured flowers several small white and yellow beads are threaded on to wire. Yellow crepe paper has been inserted between the blooms to fill the gaps.*

Bottom left: *Storm light, with chick. The dipit shapes are coated on one side with film, allowed to dry briefly and then pressed onto the outside of the glass.*

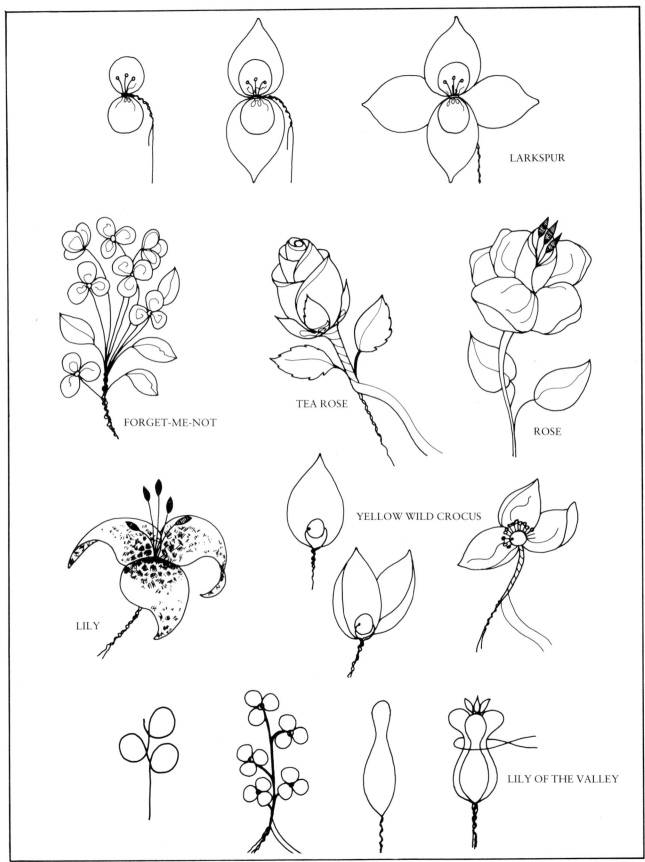

LARKSPUR

FORGET-ME-NOT

TEA ROSE

ROSE

LILY

YELLOW WILD CROCUS

LILY OF THE VALLEY

Tea roses and forget-me-nots (picture page 103)

The tea roses are made of two different-sized petals. The inner petal is rolled tight and the next one around it is shaped slightly inwards and fixed. The rest of the rose is made up of four large and two smaller yellow petals. At the base of the flower are two green leaves pointing upwards. Wind florist's tape around the stem, adding some leaves as you do so. (See sketch, page 106.)

The forget-me-nots consist of three single petals, with a white bead for the centre of each. 3–5 flowers are bound together into an umbel shape about 2cm below the flowers. Wind florist's tape around the stem, adding leaves (see sketch, page 106). The roses and forget-me-knots are mounted into Plasticine or similar foundation.

A wall decoration made of fantasy flowers intertwined around a wooden trellis.

Flower wreath: When all the flowers are made, weave the single blooms into one strip by twisting the wires around each other. Shape the flowers into a wreath and twist the end of the wire around the first bloom. You can add flowers and leaves later if there are any gaps to fill.

Jewelry

Another charming idea is to use small plastic flowers as jewelry, attached to suitable jewelry 'findings'. The jewelry may not be everlasting, but it is so cheap and easy to make that you can afford to have a matching

set for every outfit! Brooches, pendants, and bracelets are all suitable, and so are earrings, which are light and easy to wear.

Make sure you have the right chains, clips and findings before starting to make the jewelry and always use strengthener for it.

Table-wreath and napkin rings (above, top)

Make a ring out of thick wire and cover it with Plasticine. Cover the underside with aluminium foil. Insert the short-stemmed flowers made of yellow glass beads, three bright yellow and three white dip-it leaves, into the Plasticine, together with the blue buds. The golden spiral spring flowers are made as follows: take some yellow beads with silver centres, thread onto a thin

Top: a table decoration with napkin rings. The short blooms are decorated with yellow glass beads, three crocus yellow and three white plastic or resin leaves. The napkin rings are made out of self-hardening clay. The sweets container is decorated with a chain of white blooms bound tightly together.

Below: a basket of lily of the valley with yellow wild crocuses. On the right cyclamen, the centres of which have been decorated with red transparent glass paint.

thread and shape into petals. Wind silver coiled wire around the beads a number of times to give a pretty effect. The flower is finished off by joining up the individual bead petals and tying a threaded head into the centre.

Once all the flowers have been wired on the wreath, fill up the remaining gaps with green leaves.

The napkin rings are made out of self-hardening clay. Make a hole in the clay using a pencil, and then fire in an oven. Once the ring has been fired and lacquered, fill the hole with the wire ends of the short-stemmed white flowers which have been tightly bound into a bunch, and press the flower down onto the upper side of the ring. The biscuit box has also been decorated with a ring of white flowers.

Some hints and warnings

Always keep the film away from naked flames. Do not smoke while working.

Polyester solutions are highly inflammable. The working area must be ventilated.

It is not advisable to allow small children to use polyester solution or liquid film. Supervise older children. The solution must not be taken as it is toxic. If any is swallowed, call a doctor immediately.

Pale pink blooms have been painted, before being bound together, with lilac-coloured glass paint and also given black stamens.

Always replace the lid when not using the liquid film. If the liquid becomes too thick, use thinners. It is advisable to add thinners as soon as about a quarter of the can has been used, as the trapped air tends to dry the liquid.

Use newspaper or a protective covering for your work table.

Do not over-thin or the film will sag. If this happens, leave the liquid uncovered until it thickens. You can produce all sorts of shades by mixing the four primary colours, but do not mix different brands as the results may not be satisfactory.

Always dip to the top of the stem. Always allow adequate time for drying and do not touch the film before or after using the strengthener. Remember that the strengthener is a strong solution which

attacks polystyrene and other materials, so protect your working surface from drips and use potatoes for drying rather than polystyrene sheets or tiles.

You can clean these liquid film flowers with a feather duster, or you can wash them in soapy water, when they will come up like new.

If you get the solution on your hands, clothes or furniture, do not worry. It will usually peel or wash off. You may have to clean clothes, however, with acetone.

Ideas for more flowers

Basket of lily of the valley (page 108)

The wire for these blooms is twisted around a thick nail – see sketch on page 106. Once the flowers are dry, push a threaded bead through the middle of the flower towards the back and then shape the three petals so that they droop a little forwards. The

The glass flowers are enhanced by a large bead in their centre, and separately by a glass hippopotamus. The wire stems are attached to thicker wire and leaves are added at the same time as florist's tape is wound around them. Press some Plasticine onto a glass plate and insert the flower stems. Cover the Plasticine with dark blue and green leaves. String some large glass beads on to a nylon thread and use them as decoration.

flowers are fixed along the whole of the stem as shown.

Yellow wild crocus in lily-of-the-valley basket

Make the yellow crocus as shown also on page 106. Once the petals have been bound together with a thread bend the tips outwards. Plasticine is used for holding all flowers and leaves in place.

NYLON FLOWERS

NYLON FLOWERS

It is hard to believe that the enchanting flowers shown in these pages are made of discarded nylon tights and underwear! Transformed by the artistic skill of their makers, their delicate colours and shapes betray no hint of their humble origins.

This is a craft which will appeal to every creative person, and one which uses simple materials. It is also a clean craft, and so perfect for the home!

Any nylon can be used for flower-making, provided that it stretches and is not too thick. Old, laddered nylon tights or underclothes will therefore suit very well.

Even if the only nylon available is brown, the dye can be easily removed and it can be re-dyed in any colour since the range of dyes available is vast and they can be mixed to produce even subtler shades. Any dye left over can be stored in screw-top jars for use later, so the cost of dyeing can be kept to a minimum.

Usually, people are only too pleased to give away their used nylon tights. Most of us enjoy making things from what would otherwise be thrown away, and for these flowers all you need, apart from the basic material, is wire, florist's tape, wire-cutting scissors and your own patience and imagination.

Materials

Nylon tights or underwear
A reel of fine wire for binding (stocked by ironmongers)
Floristry wire for stems, 18 SWG
Silver stub wires for fine stamens (although you can use old beads with a hole large enough to be threaded with wire)
Green and white florist's tape
Small plastic plant pot saucers and other containers
Styrofoam
Moss
'Oasis-fix'
'Oasis' holders
Dress-making scissors
Wire-cutting scissors

Basic method (see Diagrams on page 113)

Always have your materials ready before you begin.

To make a tulip petal, which is the easiest and quickest petal to make, cut five lengths of flexible thin (28-gauge) florist's wire about 20cm long. Take one piece of wire and bend it into a petal shape. Hold the wire firmly together about 2cm from the end. Take a piece of nylon material and slip the wire shape inside it.

Pull the nylon around the shape of the wire and gather it at the base of the petal with your fingers. Hold the nylon firmly in place and fasten it with three turns of the reel wire. Twist the reel wire once or twice around itself to secure, then cut it free from the reel. Trim away the surplus material with dress-making scissors. Make four more petals like this.

Stamens

To make a simple stamen, take a length of flexible wire and cover it entirely with white florist's tape. Cut the wire into five equal lengths and bend one end of each piece into a small loop, which should be nipped flat. Fasten all five stamens together at the base with reel wire.

Flower assembly

Complete the petals and stamens. Take one petal at a time and attach it to the base of the stamens with reel wire. When you have positioned all five petals, secure the ends of the reel wire and trim off the excess.

Assembling the stem

Take the stiff florist's wire and bend one end of it into an open loop. Lay the loop against the base of the bunch of petals and fasten it securely with reel wire. Cover the calyx with green florist's tape. Continue down the stem until it is covered.

To increase the length of the stem, overlap two wires and join them with tape before covering the whole length. For heavy-headed flowers, use two or more wires before covering with tape. Open out the stamens and arrange them. Bend petals slightly backwards for a fully open flower or leave them a little closed for a young flower. Vary the shapes.

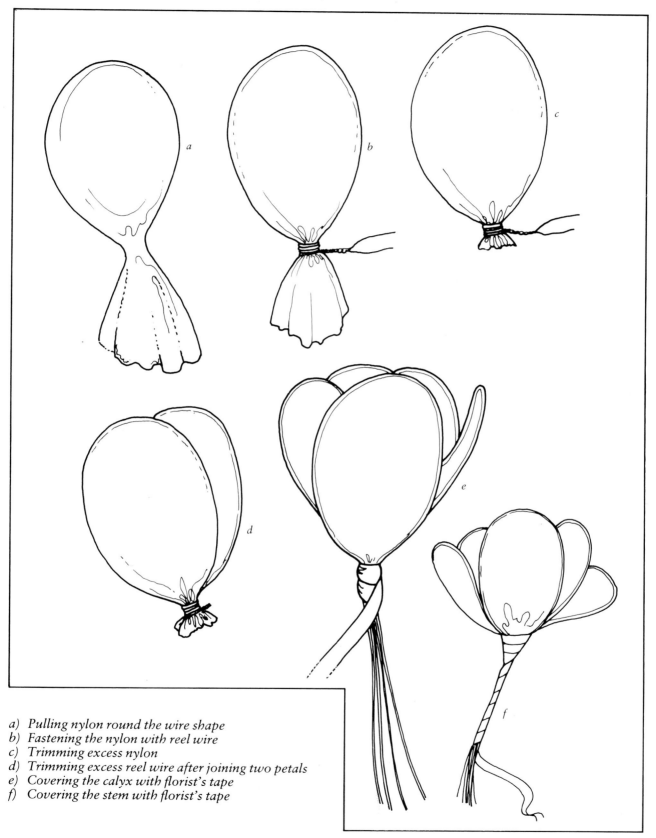

a) Pulling nylon round the wire shape
b) Fastening the nylon with reel wire
c) Trimming excess nylon
d) Trimming excess reel wire after joining two petals
e) Covering the calyx with florist's tape
f) Covering the stem with florist's tape

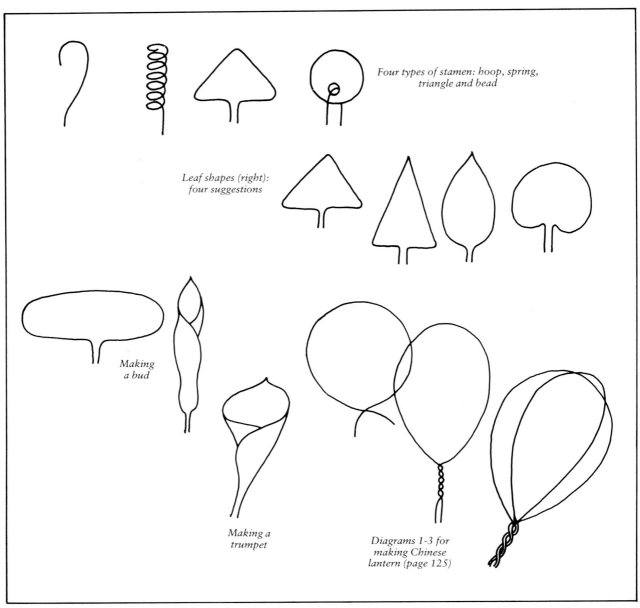

Four types of stamen: hoop, spring, triangle and bead

Leaf shapes (right): four suggestions

Making a bud

Making a trumpet

Diagrams 1-3 for making Chinese lantern (page 125)

Leaves

Dried natural materials can be used, but you also need to make some leaves. Leaf shapes, in green nylon, should be broad rather than long and thin, on the whole. Make them in the same way as petals (see the diagrams above for leaf shapes).

Buds

To form a bud, take a 20cm length of flexible wire and twist two ends around one another to prevent them slipping when you cover them with nylon. Pull the

edges of the wire out sideways until the height is about 2½cm in depth. Cover with nylon as for petals. Curl the widest part of the shape around a finger and draw it upwards to form a cone shape (see the diagram on page 120).

The flower drawings on page 116 are useful references for the shapes of different petals and the way they relate to each other. Note, too, the variations in the shapes of the stamens. Close study of flower shapes in the garden or from books, will repay you richly, for even the most vivid imagination cannot compete with the variety provided by nature.

These extraordinarily attractive winged orchids are made with mixed single-coloured and multi-coloured petals. The inner petals are twisted to make the shape more natural.

Colour variations on the petals, as in pansy hearts or on orchids, can be added with a felt-tipped pen.

Try sketching a few black and white drawings of flowers like these for yourself, and keep them in a folder with pictures cut out of magazines or seed catalogues, so that you have them by you when you start to make your nylon flowers.

Winged orchids

The flower consists of seven petals, some single-colour, some differently patterned. Between three to five petals are fixed to one stem.

Material for one flower:

Stamens: red/yellow, graduated in length. Wire loops: 1 lip petal (A) 4cm; 2 side petals (B) 5cm; 1 upper petal (C) 5cm; 1 lip petal (D) 5cm; 2 winged petals (E) 3cm. The stems are cut to lengths from 4–10cm.

Preparation

The wire loop for petal (A) is covered with orange-coloured stocking and for petal (E) with yellow

coloured stocking. All the rest are covered in white.

The markings are carried out with iron-on paints, following the basic method, as demonstrated in the illustration above, for 1–3 petals:

Circle B: large yellow, red, green and a few dark green spots.

Circle C: large yellow, red, brown, green and a few dark green spots.

Circle D: yellow and some red.

Assembly

Attach the lip petal (A) to the stamens and attach petal (D) immediately on to that. Add the petals (E) with stems next to each other, all at the same height. Then add both petals (B) on either side of the thick part and finally attach petal (C) tightly. Secure with wire and wind crepe paper around it. Press petal (A) with the stamens and petal (D) downwards. Petal (A) should be lightly waved and the upper petal somewhat rounded and turned outwards. The wings (E) should be pressed into a rather narrow shape from the base outwards and then bent outwards from the middle. The side petals (B) are pointed and slightly wavy – take them

between thumb and forefinger and bend so that one-third is facing forward and the end is bent back. Pull petal (C) into a point, leaning forwards.

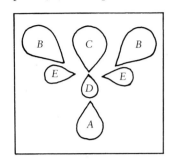

Little Red Bird of the Forest

This European wild orchid lends itself particularly well to being rendered in nylon, and is most attractive both as a stem or as a spray. The single blooms can be varied to taste, either all the same size or graduating down towards the end of the stem or along the spray. In the illustration (above) both types are made in this way and each flower has six petals.

Material for one flower

Stamen: Long and oval-shaped, red, white or yellow.
Wire loops: 6 pieces, diameter 4cm. The stems are graduated in lengths of 4–10cm.

Yellow and red orchid blossom. *The little flower on the left of the piece of weathered wood is made up of eight petals and is ideally suitable for an arrangement of 8–10 flowers. It also looks good in other colours.*

Preparation

Cover five loops with red (yellow) nylon and one loop with white (brown) nylon. Tendrils: Wind crepe paper around 25–30cm of silver wire and use a pencil to shape it into a spiral. Take the wire off the pencil and loosen the spiral by gently pulling it.
Fixing: Attach the red flowers to a double thickness stem. On the yellow spray start with the smallest bud. Add small and large green leaves to alternate with the tendrils and blooms without extra wire support.

Blue blooms (Bunny's ears)

The inspiration for these blossoms came from a half-open bloom of creeping forget-me-nots. Each flower has five single petals.

Material for one flower

Stamen: Yellow and red-yellow, mixed.
Wire: 3 pieces 3½cm, one piece 6cm, one piece 2½cm. For the two 'Bunny's ears' 25cm of 6mm strong silver wire.

Preparation

The finest wires are left bare; the others are covered in blue nylon. Out of the wire make two connected 'ears' 4½cm long, as shown in the picture (right),

which can be covered with blue nylon. To hold them in the middle use reel wire; tighten and cover with crepe paper.

To finish

Bind together one small blue leaf and one white one. Join the stamens to them and place the small blue leaves and the 'bunny's ears' on the same level. Press down the white leaf together with the blue, and bend the 'ears' upwards. Mould the two side leaves like butterfly wings and arrange the large blue leaf behind the thick part. Press them together, bend half round and shape so that a rounded end lies between the 'ears' and on both sides. Fix on the finished flowers and either bend the blooms forward or level backwards.

A colourful posy. You can use dazzling colours and many different flower shapes to put together this posy. The white flowers with one orange-red petal can be made by following the instructions opposite for Bunny's ears. You will also know how to make the spray of orchids. The only new flower is the 'tuerkenbund' lily, where each blossom is made up of six petals.

Stylised nylon and apple-tray flowers

You can make attractive stylised flowers from the dimpled plastic trays used for packing apples.

Cover them with nylon. White trays are best but if you can only obtain coloured ones, paint them first with white emulsion paint. Do not use aerosol paint spray as this may destroy the plastic.

Cut six dimples from the apple tray and shave one end of each to make a petal shape. Cover each petal with nylon, and wire them together with reel wire to form a flower. Make spring-shaped stamens by winding lengths of thin wire covered in florist's tape around a knitting needle. To make leaves, cover dimples with green nylon and attach a length of wire at the base for attaching to the stem.

Lady's Slipper. *This variety of orchid displays the most subtle of colours and markings. The colour on the actual 'shoe' or 'lip' is repeated in clear but differently drawn markings on the side and upper petals. This flower has altogether eight petals.*

120

*A group of delicate orchids in variegated stripes
looks perfectly natural on a setting of gnarled wood.
Note how closely the artist has kept to the colours
and designs of real flowers.*

Other realistic flowers

Roses

When making roses, grade the size of the petals from the centre outwards. Two smallish petals in the middle surrounded by three slightly larger ones, with five even larger petals on the outside.

Make sure the petals overlap, and bend them into natural shapes. You can add oval-shaped leaves to the stem, one near the top of the stem and two facing each other lower down the stem. For the rosebuds, form a longish head, and then three smaller shapes with only 20cm length of wire and six leaves of normal size with 25cm length of wire. The head comes in the middle of the three petals which are pulled together with the first wire. Then fasten together three leaves each with the second and third wire. When joined, the single leaves will each lie partly over the previous leaf.

Daffodils

Make five slightly elongated petals for the outside and one for the central trumpet. Make the trumpet in the same way as a bud but when rolling it around your finger, do not draw it out into a cone. The trum-pet can be the same colour as the petals or a deeper shade of orange. You cannot copy natural daffodil leaves in nylon, so use arrowhead leaves instead.

Snowdrops

Make them from three small oval-shaped petals and one central trumpet. Group the three outside petals around the trumpet and bend them slightly outwards at the tip. Attach the flower head to the stem in a drooping position.

Iris

Make this from six petals – three central ones, narrow and pointed and arranged upwards, and three wider outside petals that hang downwards. Omit the trum-pet of the natural iris as it makes the artificial flower look too heavy.

Sweet peas

Made from three petals of varying sizes. One large semi-circular one for the back of the flower, a medium-sized half-moon petal for the middle, and a small triangular one for the front of the flower. Attach five or more flowers to a single stem.

Narcissi

Make these the same way as daffodils, except that the trumpet should be shorter and the petals should be slightly wider. Try joining two or three heads onto a single stem, with small flowers. Nip the ends of the outside petals into points.

Freesias

Make some buds at the top of the stem from small pieces of hoop-shaped wire covered with green nylon. The partly-opened flowers are made from small curled trumpets and the open flowers from larger trumpets with wider openings. Bend the stem wire at a right angle after the addition of each flower and bud, so that the stem has a zigzag appearance as in the real flower.

Arum lilies

Make these from one very large petal. Twist the ends of the wire together before covering with nylon in order to maintain its shape and position. The stamen is made from a long, thin hoop of wire covered in white florist's tape. Wire the stamen and the petal together and form the petal into a trumpet-shape around the stamen. Nip the top of the trumpet to a point.

Primroses

The real primrose has five petals but three will look just as realistic. The stamen is one small, straight wire in the centre of the petals. Use plenty of buds and shape the leaves as in the natural flower.

Gladioli

In the real flower there are always buds and unopened flowers at the top of the spike, so imitate this feature. Make the buds from two small oval sepals covered with green nylon. Wire them together face to face. For an opening flower, make two more sepals and wire a petal, slightly larger than the sepals, between them, so that it just emerges. Attach the buds and opening flowers alternately on either side at the top of your stem wire. You need five flowers to make a spectacular gladiolus, and these are made from five diamond-shaped petals wired around a hoop-shaped stamen which just emerges at the centre. Open out the petals flat round the stamen. Use more than one stem wire before covering with florist's tape. Split the stem at the bottom when mounting the flower in a Styrofoam base to make it stand safely.

Montbretias

These flowers are particularly useful in small arrangements, when they can be used to give height at the back. They can also give flowing lines when bent sideways. Like freesias, the spiky flowers open at varying times, so add some buds at the top of the

stems. The flowers are made from five small diamond-shaped hoops joined around a small, hoop-shaped stamen covered with florist's tape. Once the petals are attached to the stamen, arrange them to form a star shape.

Anemones. *These anemones are made in the same basic way as described on pages 112–13, but the stamens around the flat centre can be chosen to blend with the various petal colours. Anemones grow wild in the woods in springtime and their delicate rosy blooms can be seen peeping out from under a mass of dark green leaves. Although they grow in profusion, they are frequently ignored by walkers.*

A charmingly unusual arrangement of nylon foxgloves mixed with real ferns. The foxgloves are individually made in pink dyed nylon with long stamens. They are wired on to a long stem of double wire, to support the weight of so many blooms.

Harebells are made in a similar way to the foxgloves, the only difference being the way in which the petals are fixed: these are all placed at the same height and also the stem is finished with green leaves made of stocking material.

attractive details. Thus the iris, for instance, can be made in three ways:

1. Add three pistils in the middle, as for lilies.
2. Make a thin, elongated flower centre, as for a rose, but thinner and longer.
3. Make three small petal shapes out of thinner wire than for the larger shapes, but in the same colour as the larger petals underneath. However, if you wish the flower to be in one colour only, then the markings on the three small petals in the middle, should be in a different colour.

In nature iris petals are large so you must work with longer pieces of wire. If you plan to make several flowers of the same kind, prepare all the petals at the same time.

The flower cluster on the left of the illustration, is worked from the top downwards. Take two small 'buttons' as buds (Diagrams 4 and 5) and add a smaller flower to the stem, followed by a green leaf. As you work your way down the stem vary the flower size, making it bigger towards the bottom, and at intervals add a green leaf or a bud with a leaf on an adjoining stem.

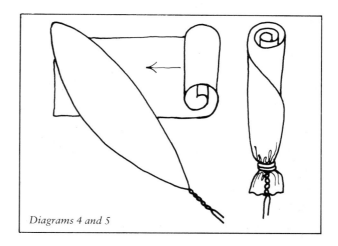

Diagrams 4 and 5

Chinese lantern

Twist two 25cm long wires together into loops (Diags. 1, 2; p. 114) and separate them so that they cross each other at right angles as in Diagram 3. The nylon used is orange. The covered lanterns are attached to a branch, bamboo or a strong piece of wire, pointing downwards – hence the name lantern. This can be made with or without leaves as a large or small bush, according to requirements. The finished example shown in the illustration (above) is 52cm high.

Flower arrangement with irises (see next page)

There is no need to reproduce the actual flowers exactly. You can let your imagination run free and add

The smaller seed flower cluster on the right of the illustration is started with a small bell-shaped flower made up of only two petals which lean downwards and a tight bud in the middle. The next one has four petals and some green leaves. As an alternative, butter-cups or forget-me-nots look good with irises. The waterlily is white, but could also be a delicate pink or yellow. In its centre is a flat yellow knob. You can make it either with three or with six petals. Its green leaves are extra large, made of 50cm lengths of wire.

125

Arrangement

Once all the flower clusters and leaves are made, you can start building up the arrangement. Begin with the largest and tallest flowers, the iris, the mauve/yellow flowers and bullrushes. If you cannot find these in a flower shop, you can look for them on the shores of a lake or pond edge. Alternatively, use gladioli leaves. The fresh leaves are placed on a pile of absorbent paper (unprinted newsprint) and pressed with an iron. To protect the iron, cover the leaves with paper as well. Then store the leaves between two sheets of packing paper. They should be dyed with green wood-stain.

The yellow cluster (left) is the same height as the second iris (right) then the red cluster is placed at a lower level than the iris. Make sure these are firmly secured before adding the first waterlily leaf. Having added the second leaf, and the waterlily itself, the third leaf is used to hold the flower and leaves in place. When the arrangement is complete, put it into a ball of Plasticine or some plaster and then into a container.

Cleaning nylon flowers

You can wash nylon flowers so long as you make sure they are quickly and thoroughly dried. They tend to rust only where the wire has been left uncovered. Flowers incorporating apple-tray petals should be dry-cleaned.

OTHER CRAFT TITLES

DECORATING CAKES FOR CHILDREN'S PARTIES
by Polly Pinder

Thirty-one cakes tastefully illustrated in full colour plus 424 step-by-step drawings that will inspire the reader to make these stunning and delightful cakes. Cake ideas include Humpty Dumpty, Superman, Winnie-the-Pooh, Fast-food addict.

HOMEMADE and at a fraction of the cost
by Polly Pinder

'An imaginative and practical book full of ideas, recipes and instructions for making breads, chutneys, drinks, sweets, soft cheese, soaps. Superb colour photographs.' *The Lady*. Cased and paperback.

MADE TO TREASURE
Embroideries for all Occasions edited by Kit Pyman.

This book offers a rich variety of ideas for embroideries to be made to commemorate special occasions – christenings, weddings, birthdays – from simple greetings cards to a gold-work panel for a golden wedding. A heart warming present precisely because it is specially made.

THE SPLENDID SOFT TOY BOOK

The Splendid Soft Toy Book contains a wealth of ideas and pictures for making a wide variety of toys and dolls, from a green corduroy crocodile to detailed traditional, even collectors' dolls. More than 60 full colour pictures and over 70 black and white illustrations show the reader how to fashion appealing figures and animals of all shapes and sizes. Cased and paperback.

THE CHRISTMAS CRAFTS BOOK

Creative ideas and designs for the whole family to make objects with a Christmas flavour: table and room decorations, stars, Christmas tree ornaments, candles and candlesticks, angels, nativity scenes, paper chains and Christmas cards.

EVERY KIND OF PATCHWORK
edited by Kit Pyman

'Really lives up to its title, and is sufficiently easy to follow that even the most helpless needleperson would be tempted to have a go. But there's plenty, too, for the experienced.' *The Guardian*. Cased and Paperback.

MAGNIFICENT PATCHWORK
by Marie-Janine Solvit

For every needlecraft enthusiast. 50 original designs for bedspreads, cushions, wall-hangings, and many other useful items for the home.

COLOURCRAFT

Hundreds of simple ideas, designs and ways of using colour to express your natural creativity and imagination.

NATURECRAFT

A crafts book for all who love the colour, shape and texture of natural materials.

If you are interested in any of the above books or any of the art and craft titles published by Search Press please send for free catalogue to: Search Press Ltd., Dept B, Wellwood, North Farm Road, Tunbridge Wells, Kent. TN2 3DR.